Bats of Florida

UNIVERSITY PRESS OF FLORIDA

Florida A&M University, Tallahassee
Florida Atlantic University, Boca Raton
Florida Gulf Coast University, Ft. Myers
Florida International University, Miami
Florida State University, Tallahassee
University of Central Florida, Orlando
University of Florida, Gainesville
University of North Florida, Jacksonville
University of South Florida, Tampa
University of West Florida, Pensacola

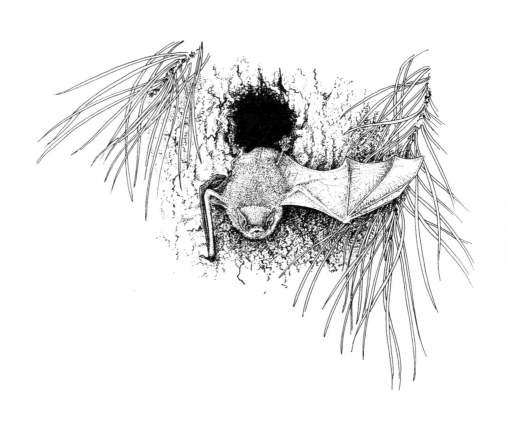

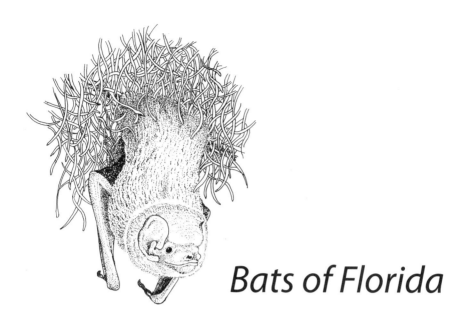

Bats of Florida

Cynthia S. Marks and George E. Marks

Drawings by Tom McOwat

University Press of Florida
Gainesville/Tallahassee/Tampa/Boca Raton
Pensacola/Orlando/Miami/Jacksonville/Ft. Myers

Copyright 2006 by Cynthia S. and George E. Marks
Printed in Canada on acid-free paper

11 10 09 08 07 06   6 5 4 3 2 1

A record of cataloging-in-publication data is available from the
Library of Congress.
ISBN 0-8130-2985-6

The University Press of Florida is the scholarly publishing agency
for the State University System of Florida, comprising Florida A&M
University, Florida Atlantic University, Florida Gulf Coast University,
Florida International University, Florida State University, University
of Central Florida, University of Florida, University of North Florida,
University of South Florida, and University of West Florida.

University Press of Florida
15 Northwest 15th Street
Gainesville, FL 32611-2079
http://www.upf.com

Contents

Preface

Florida is famous for its birds, alligators, dolphins, sea turtles, and fish, but few people are aware of its wide diversity of bats. Yet, shortly after sunset each night, when most birds have gone to roost, Florida's skies become host to the world's only flying mammals—bats. Almost invisible in the night skies, they often go unnoticed. When seen, they appear as mysterious fluttering shadows and reveal little of their true size and shape, or their mission in the night sky. Because they are small, reclusive, flighted, and nocturnal, they are difficult to study. This, coupled with myths, rumor, and countless fictional distortions, has caused bats to be among the last of the mammals to be studied, and likely the most misunderstood. Hence, through no fault of their own, these small, furry, nonaggressive, and intelligent creatures go about their evening activities, exterminating thousands of insects, while humans below remain unaware of their presence or, worse, on seeing them, react with fear and loathing.

This picture is changing. Many people are becoming aware of bats, their place in natural ecosystems, and their benefits to those around them. Our purpose in writing this book is to provide an introduction to bats in general, a resource on the bats of Florida for those who have a personal desire to learn more, and a reference for those who work with bats. We became interested in bats in 1989 and were quickly captivated by their unusual characteristics, amazing behaviors, and wide diversity. Since then we have been rescuing bats, working on conservation projects, conducting field surveys, and helping people with bats in buildings, accumulating a great deal of experience and information along the way. In 1994, we established the Florida Bat Center (now the Florida Bat Conservancy), a nonprofit organization dedicated to conserving native bat populations in Florida. We, along with many faithful volunteers, are working on various bat-related projects and caring for numerous bats that have been injured or orphaned. During the past fifteen years, we have presented well over 1,000 educational programs about bats. In the course of our work, we have met many people who were initially fearful of bats, and others who viewed them with contempt, but in nearly all cases, after a brief introduction to bats, they left with a wonder and appreciation for these amazing animals. It is our goal that this book will convey that same wonder and appreciation to its readers.

Acknowledgments

We take this opportunity to thank the many individuals whose assistance and cooperation have been invaluable to us in the preparation of this book. We are especially grateful to Jeff Gore for providing information and suggestions throughout the project and for many lengthy discussions on Florida bats. We are also especially thankful to Ted Fleming for sharing information from his personal research, answering numerous questions regarding Caribbean bat species, and making valuable suggestions on the manuscript.

Much of the information on bat species in the Florida Keys is based on data gathered through numerous trips to Key West over a five-year period. Our success would not have been possible without the help of one very special person, Fran Ford. A long-time leader in conservation for the area, Fran knows just about everyone associated with wildlife in the Florida Keys. Whatever information or assistance we needed, Fran was able to provide it, or direct us to someone who could. Through her we met many people who have helped us or provided leads on bat sightings in the Keys. We especially treasure our time with Fran's husband, Commander William Ford, whose humor, hospitality, and conversations are always a delight. We are grateful for the help of the following people in Key West: Homer Herrick, Darlene Pruess, Danny Soldano, Pat Rogers, Sarah and Steve Baxter, Andrew Hearn, Tony Barroso, Karen Wray, Phyllis Pope, Jackie McCorkle, Carolann Sharkey, and Misha McRae. For assistance in other parts of the Florida Keys, we thank Donna Sprunt, Miriam Goode, Phil Frank, Jim Dusquenel, Patricia Mull, and the staff at the Audubon Tavernier Science Center. Our thanks to each of you, and we hope to see you again as we continue our work with bats in the Florida Keys.

We are indebted to Thor Holmes at the University of Kansas Natural History Museum and to Don Wilson at the Smithsonian's National Museum of Natural History for re-examining specimens in their respective museum collections. Also, we thank Laurie Wilkins, Candace McCaffery, and David Reed at the Florida Museum of Natural History for helping us locate and examine specimens.

We especially thank Jerome Jackson for his thorough review of the manuscript and his many helpful suggestions. Others we wish to thank for reviewing all, or parts, of the manuscript and providing comments and suggestions are John Fitch, Charles Rupprecht, Bob Timm, and Ken Glover.

We are indebted to Tom McOwat for illustrating our book with his excellent artwork. We are also grateful to Scott Altenbach for providing many of the color photos, and to all of our other photographers—Barry Mansell, Courtney Platt, Jeff Gore, and Stan Kirkland—for the use of their photographs.

Board members and volunteers of the Florida Bat Conservancy have helped in many ways. Bill and Sarah Kern provided information and assisted in field work. Ken Arrison read early drafts of the manuscript and reviewed them for content and flow. Ann Walker proofed the early manuscript, adding a multitude of commas. George Fenner assisted with the design of the bat house plans and, along with his wife Lupe, translated reference material on Cuban bat species. We also thank Nancy Douglas, Polly and Calvin Kimball, Tish Thomas, and Nita Claytor for their support while we worked on this project.

Other people we would like to thank include Carlos Mancina, for information on Cuban species; Roy Marks and Laura Manson, for their input on difficult grammatical questions; Susan Trokey and Victor Young, for information and monitoring of the Florida bonneted bats in their bat house; Steve Barlow, for information on the large community bat houses he has constructed on wildlife management areas and refuges in Florida; Maria Calcaterra and Pam Colarusso, for data on bats submitted for rabies testing; Lois Blumenthal, for information on bats in the Cayman Islands; Karl Studenroth, for information on bats in bridges; Suzanne Banas, for rescuing and caring for the buffy flower bat found in Miami; Terry Doonan, for information on museum specimens; Gary Morgan, for information on Florida's fossil records; Betty Reardon and Wes Brookes, for discovering and photographing the Cuban fig-eating bat in the Key West Tropical Forest and Botanical Gardens; Judith Burhman, for assistance in finding research papers; Christina Evans, for help with graphics software; and Chico (our cockatiel), for perforating the edges of all of our papers while we worked.

We never would have become involved with bats if it had not been for Bat Conservation International (BCI). So, we must take this opportunity to thank Merlin Tuttle for founding BCI and, through it, introducing us to the world of bats. We also want to thank Brock Fenton for conveying the wonder of these amazing animals to us at our first workshop in 1990 and for continuing to inspire us at subsequent workshops and conferences.

1

Biology of Bats

Worldwide there are more than 1,000 species of bats, making bats one of the most diverse and widespread groups of mammals on earth. Bats constitute 20 percent, or one-fifth, of the world's mammalian species. Bats are found on all continents of the world except Antarctica and have colonized all but the most remote oceanic islands. They have adapted to all climates except those of extreme desert and polar regions. As with many other animals, the greatest diversity and abundance of bat species occur in tropical regions and decline as one progresses to more temperate areas.

Bats are unique among mammals, their most significant distinction being that they are the only mammals to have achieved true flight. Other "flying" mammals, such as flying squirrels or flying lemurs, are only able to glide—a significant feat in itself, but not true flight. Bats, like birds, can sustain flight under their own power for extended periods of time. A second distinction is that, for their size, bats are the longest-lived of the mammals. Big brown bats, which weigh less than an ounce, can live for more than thirty years, a remarkable lifespan for such a small animal. Also, for their size, bats are the slowest reproducing of mammals. Most female bats give birth to only one pup per year. Another amazing accomplishment is the development of a sophisticated form of biosonar commonly referred to as "echolocation." The adaptive capabilities, specializations, and resulting diversity of these small mammals are nothing less than astounding.

Classification

In the 1700s, when animals were first being scientifically classified, it was determined that bats were sufficiently unique among mammals to be placed in a separate order. The order was labeled Chiroptera, which literally means "hand-wing." The order Chiroptera was then divided into two suborders: Megachiroptera and Microchiroptera. Today, bats within these two suborders are frequently referred to as megabats and microbats. As the names imply, the two suborders consist generally of large bats and small bats, respectively. The suborder Megachiroptera, however, includes only a single family of bats, the Pteropodidae,

Table 1.1. Classification of Bats Compared to Humans

	Evening bats	Humans
Kingdom	Animalia	Animalia
Phylum	Chordata	Chordata
Class	Mammalia	Mammalia
Order	Chiroptera	Primates
Suborder	Microchiroptera	—
Family	Vespertilionidae	Hominidae
Genus	*Nycticeius*	*Homo*
Species	*Nycticeius humeralis*	*Homo sapiens*

often referred to as "flying foxes" because of their long, foxlike faces. Mega-chiropteran bats (Pteropodidae) are found only in the Old World tropics, encompassing the tropical areas of Africa, Asia, Australia, and the Pacific Islands. Because of their range and their diet, they are also often referred to as the "Old World fruit bats." The suborder Microchiroptera, on the other hand, currently consists of seventeen families representing a huge diversity of bat species. Unlike megabats, microchiropteran bats are found on all continents of the world with the exception of Antarctica. All species of bats in the New World (and hence Florida) are microchiropteran bats.

The above classification of bats stood for nearly 300 years. Then in the late 1980s the classification was challenged on several fronts. Recent discoveries at that time suggested that perhaps megachiropteran and microchiropteran bats had evolved from two different ancestors, each of which had independently developed "hand-wings" and the ability to fly. Other evidence supported the traditional thinking that they had descended from a single ancestor. At one point it was even postulated that the megabats should be reclassified as primates. The general feeling was that it would require molecular biology (the study of genetics) to unravel the mystery. Following the 1980s, additional studies created a growing body of evidence that once again led to the conclusion that bats evolved from a single, but yet unknown, ancestor. Molecular studies, however, reveal a more complex arrangement than the simplified concept of megabats and microbats. Investigations to date are showing that some microbat families are more closely related to megabats than to the other microbats. As a result, a new grouping of bats is being considered, but more work is needed before the final arrangement can be determined.

Over the past years, the official count of bat species has risen from 925 in 1993 to 1,116 in 2005. Of the increase, most newly defined species were the result of reclassification of existing species, based on new studies and using new technologies. Only about a quarter of the increase was due to the discovery of a

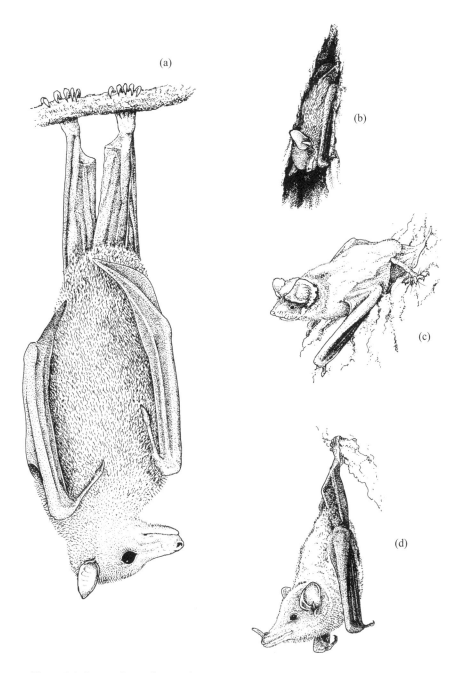

Figure 1.1. Comparison of megachiropteran and microchiropteran bats. (a) Megachiropteran bat (family Pteropodidae). Examples of three microchiropteran families: (b)
Vespertilionidae, (c) Molossidae, and (d) Phyllostomidae.

previously unknown bat species. It is inevitable the number will change again as new species are discovered and existing ones are reclassified. Although there are many differences in the physical makeup and behaviors of the 1,116 species of bats, they all have one thing in common: flight. When comparing the anatomy of bats to that of other mammals, one finds that although the biological components are basically the same, many have been modified in some way to facilitate flight. Most of these adaptations are unique among mammals, adding to the wonder and mystery of these amazing animals.

Flight

It has not been determined how bats first achieved flight because fossils linking bats to an early nonflighted mammal have yet to be found. The most generally accepted theory, however, is that the ancient ancestors of bats were likely small arboreal (tree-dwelling) mammals that began early flight experiences by jumping from tree branch to tree branch. Extensions of the skin from the body to the arms and legs, combined with webbing between the fingers, would have proven helpful and enabled this animal to glide greater distances than could be achieved by simply jumping. By adding downward strokes of the forearms during the glide, it would have been possible to further extend the distance traveled. Adjustments to wing structure over time through the evolutionary process likely maximized what could be achieved using a basic mammalian hand-wing configuration. It appears that the optimum configuration has been accomplished, since the wing structure of bats today is essentially the same as that found in bat fossils more than 50 million years old. It is possible that the evolutionary process occurred rapidly, since flight provides decided advantages. Anything that would enhance the ability to move from tree to tree without expending time and energy to run down one and up the other and, more importantly, without exposing oneself to terrestrial predators, would greatly increase the chances of survival. Although flight requires roughly twice as much energy per unit of time as running, it consumes only one-fifth the energy per unit of distance traveled. Such an accomplishment would greatly expand the foraging capabilities of this small mammal and, as insectivorous bats obviously discovered, it would also open up a new and previously unobtainable source of food: flying insects. The advantages of true flight are significant, but achieving it is difficult. Numerous specialized modifications have occurred in the anatomy of bats to make it possible.

If humans had designed the bat's wing it would be touted as an engineering marvel. Beginning with something similar to a human hand, bats have evolved a complex system of bone, tissue, and muscle that meets the aerodynamic requirements for true flight. Since bats do not have hollow bones and feathers to reduce weight and gain lift, they must constantly support flight through their own muscle power. Individual components of the hand-wing work together as a system, providing remarkable power, efficiency, and flexibility. Elongated forearm and fingers are connected by a thin, but tough, membrane running from finger to finger and along the bat's body to its ankle (figure 1.2). This wing membrane, also called the patagium, is made up of the bat's skin and contains within it thin muscles and tiny blood vessels. The large area of the wing connecting the fifth finger, arm, body, and hind leg is called the plagiopatagium and provides most of the lift needed for flight. The outward portion of the wing membrane connecting the second through fifth fingers is called the chiropatagium. This area of the wing provides most of the forward thrust and has great flexibility in form and shape. The leading edge of the wing is formed by the portion of the chiropatagium connecting the second and third fingers, and a small membrane in front of the arm, called the propatagium. The pitch (angle) of these two membranes can be altered using the thumb and second finger. By adjusting their leading edge downward, the bat can prevent stalling at high angles of attack (orientation of wing to airflow) and preserve lift at low flight speeds. Lowering these membranes and arching the fifth finger changes the overall camber of the wing. Increasing wing camber increases lift at the expense of drag, a necessary trade-off during portions of the wing beat and certain flight maneuvers.

A number of bat species also have a posterior membrane connecting the hind legs and encompassing the tail. This membrane, the uropatagium, is commonly referred to as the tail membrane. The tail membrane is normally extended during flight, providing additional lift. The bat can alter the orientation of the tail membrane with its legs and use it as an aid in steering. By dropping its hind feet, the bat can block the air flow and use the tail membrane as a brake. Some insectivorous bats also use the tail membrane as a handy tool for capturing insects in flight.

Bats have seventeen muscles involved in the movement of each wing. Of these, four play a primary role in the downstroke and four in the upstroke. The other nine muscles are used to change the shape of the wing and maintain tension on wing membranes. It is evident the flight of bats is considerably more complex than that of fixed-wing aircraft and a great deal more flexible than that of birds. The geometry of the wing is recurrently altered during the wingbeat cycle and abruptly modified as needed to maneuver and capture insect prey in the air.

The wings of bat species are also highly specialized to complement their respective lifestyles. Bats that forage for flying insects in open areas need to be fast fliers. Bats that forage around trees and undergrowth, or that pluck insects

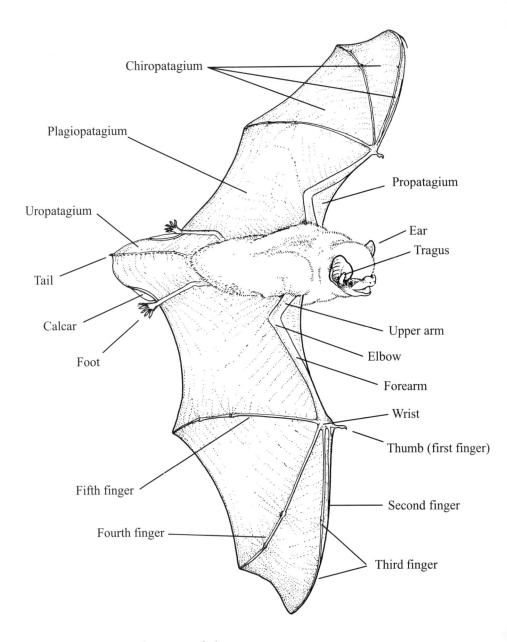

Chiropatagium

Plagiopatagium

Propatagium

Uropatagium

Ear

Tragus

Tail

Calcar

Upper arm

Foot

Elbow

Forearm

Wrist

Thumb (first finger)

Fifth finger

Second finger

Fourth finger

Third finger

Figure 1.2. External anatomy of a bat.

off the ground or stationary objects, need maneuverability. Other bats may need something in between. A single wing design cannot optimally serve all of these needs. Consequently, individual species of bats have developed wing configurations that best meet their specific needs. Two terms are helpful in comparing the wings of bats. Wing loading is a measure of how much weight the wings are being required to bear. It is calculated by dividing the weight of the bat by the total surface area of the wing membrane. A heavy bat with small wings would therefore have a high wing loading. The second term, aspect ratio, is a measure of the length of a wing compared to its width. For regularly shaped wings, like those of airplanes, it can be calculated simply as the wingspan divided by the wing width. For irregularly shaped wings, like those of bats, it is best calculated as the wingspan squared, divided by the surface area of the wings. Consequently, bats with long narrow wings have a high aspect ratio. Just like high-speed aircraft, fast-flying bats such as the Brazilian free-tailed bat have wings with high aspect ratios and high wing loadings. They fly fast and forage in open areas at speeds of 30–50 mph. Rafinesque's big-eared bat, on the other hand, flies within forested areas, gleaning insects from trees and foliage, and therefore needs high maneuverability more than speed. It has large broad wings with both low wing loading and low aspect ratio. Observers have been amazed as they watch this bat flying close to the ground, circling stationary objects and even hovering in place. Most other bats in Florida lie somewhere in between. To some extent, it is possible to make inferences about the foraging strategy of a bat simply by studying the configuration of its wings.

Circulatory System

Accomplishing sustained flight requires huge amounts of energy. The circulatory system is the pipeline that distributes oxygen, nutrients, hormones, and antibodies to the organs and tissues demanding them, and receives carbon dioxide and waste products for elimination. The heart is responsible for keeping all of these flowing and for matching the flow to the rapidly changing demands on the bat's circulatory system. Meeting the needs of a flying mammal presents a challenge that can be matched only by a very unusual heart. In relation to their size, bats have the largest and most muscular heart of any mammal. Individual muscle fibers within it are thinner than those of most mammals, allowing a denser volume of muscle tissue and more powerful contractions. The heart of a bat weighs 2–3 times that of a similar-sized, nonflying mammal. The volume of blood pumped per stroke (for its size) is not that different from other mammals, but the maximum rates and the ability to abruptly change those rates are nothing less than phenomenal. A bat at normal body temperature has a heart

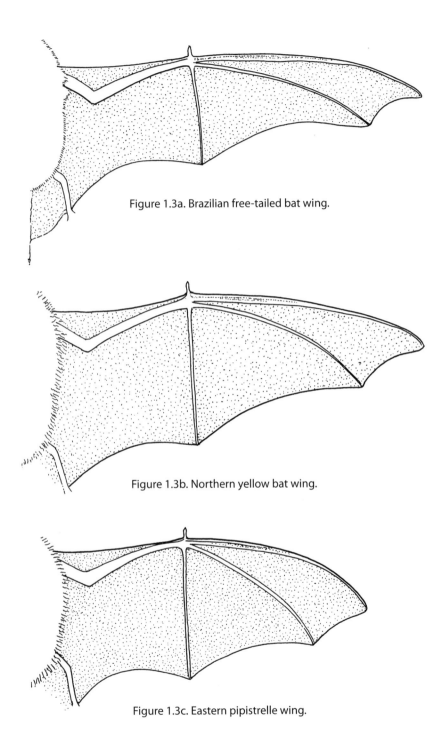

Figure 1.3a. Brazilian free-tailed bat wing.

Figure 1.3b. Northern yellow bat wing.

Figure 1.3c. Eastern pipistrelle wing.

rate of about 450 beats per minute. During hibernation, the heart rate drops to as low as 4 beats per minute. When a bat takes flight, the heart rate can jump to more than 1,000 beats per minute!

Wing membranes, being made of living tissue, also require a supply of blood and therefore contain arteries, veins, and capillaries. As the wings of bats rapidly flap up and down, centrifugal forces tend to drive the blood away from the heart. This, coupled with the fact that the wingtips are a long distance from the heart to begin with, creates a problem for which the bats have developed yet another unique adaptation. The smooth muscles within the walls of the blood vessels of the wings not only contract tonically (steadily to resist stretching) as in other mammals; they also contract peristaltically (rhythmically in a wavelike action). This action takes place to some extent in the arteries of the wing membrane but occurs more frequently and more powerfully in the veins. Because of this unique pumping action, the blood vessels in the wings of bats have been referred to as *Venenherzen* or "venous hearts," another amazing adaptation to support flight.

Hind Legs

Apparently, one of the sacrifices made by bats as they adapted to flight was the reduced size and muscle strength of their hind legs. Although bats can use their feet for crawling, the feet are relatively small and more specialized for hanging and for supporting the uropatagium in flight. The legs are rotated opposite to that of other mammals, with the knees facing toward the rear, rather than forward. This reverses the toes to facilitate hanging and enables the bat to cup the tail membrane to use it as a brake or to capture insects in flight. On the downside, it makes it impossible for the bat to walk upright on all fours like other mammals. This is not a big disadvantage when climbing backward up into a roost, but on a horizontal surface, bats are forced to crawl in an awkward spider-like manner. The feet of bats have five toes with sharp claws able to grip onto all but the smoothest of surfaces. Muscles are able to maneuver the individual toes into a variety of positions to assist grasping irregular surfaces. Once the toes have gripped a surface, a tendon-locking mechanism in the leg is activated by the bat's body weight, allowing it to hang without using any muscles and, hence, not expending any energy. This is similar to the mechanism allowing birds to sleep while perched. Unique to bats is the development of a cartilaginous spur called the calcar. The calcar protrudes from the ankle and supports the outer edge of the tail membrane (uropatagium; figure 1.2). This feature adds rigidity to the tail membrane, increasing its surface area during flight. Some calcars are "keeled," having a flattened area extending beyond the trailing edge. Often when

Figure 1.4. The hind legs of bats are reversed, with the knees facing to the rear.

species are very similar, the presence or absence of a calcar and whether or not it is keeled can be important factors aiding identification.

Hearing

Because of their dependence on echolocation, hearing is of extreme importance to microchiropteran bats. Hearing is also important for the detection of predators, and some species use it to hear the sounds made by their prey. The basic structure of a bat's ear is essentially the same as that of other mammals, but the cochlea of microchiropteran bats is modified to enhance the accuracy of their echolocation. The cochlea is a small spiral-shaped organ within the inner ear that looks much like a snail shell. Within the cochlea are fluid-filled tubes lined with hairlike cells. Frequencies of incoming sounds are detected by the hair cells, with higher frequencies being detected near the base or beginning of the spiral and lower frequencies at its end, near the apex or center of the spiral. The ability to distinguish between frequencies is a function of the gradient (change) in hair cell lengths and membrane stiffness from the beginning to the end of the spiral. An animal with a cochlea of three turns would have more frequency discrimination than one with two turns. In microchiropteran bats, the cochlea has two and a half to three turns, while in megabats and primates it has one and three-quarter turns. To accommodate the additional turns, the cochlea is proportionally larger in microchiropteran bats than in other mammals, allowing the length of the spiral to be extended within the frequency range of their echolocation calls.

Because returning echoes are extremely faint, many bats have developed large and unusually shaped ears. Generally, bats with high intensity calls have normal-sized ears, and bats with low intensity calls have larger ears. A feature

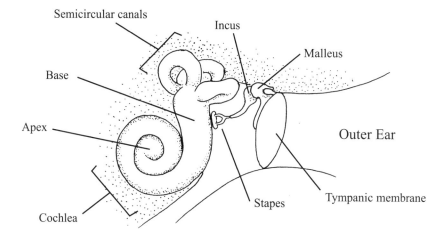

Figure 1.5. Anatomy of the inner ear.

unique to microbats is a fleshy structure in the lower front opening of the ear, called the tragus (figure 1.2). The tragus varies greatly in size and shape among species and is often an important characteristic used for identification. The tragus modifies the incoming sound waves in a manner that enhances the bat's ability to assess the vertical direction of the source of the sound.

Teeth

The teeth of bat species vary and are adapted to match their respective diets. Four types of teeth are found in bats: incisors, canines, premolars, and molars. Insectivorous bats have sharp teeth designed for chewing through the exoskeletons of their insect prey. Their incisors (front teeth) are usually small, while canine teeth are relatively long. Their molars have cusps shaped in a way that enables them to chew prey rapidly, through a combination of cutting and crushing motions. Carnivorous bats show little modification from that of insectivorous bats. This may support the theory that carnivorous diets evolved from insectivorous ones. Frugivorous bats have flattened tooth surfaces, especially the surfaces of the molars, a design that works well for chewing fruit. Nectarivorous bats have little need of teeth at all and their molars are greatly reduced, rounded, and rootless. The only teeth that remain large are the canines. The bottom incisors are absent and the top incisors are reduced and usually separated, allowing the tongue to reach between them. Vampire bats are equipped

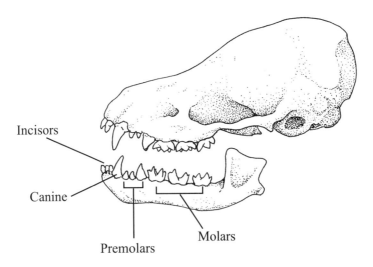

Figure 1.6. Dentition of a typical insectivorous bat.

with razor sharp incisors, which effectively clip off a small piece of skin before they begin to lap up their meal of blood from the open wound. The common vampire (*Desmodus rotundus*) has only 20 teeth and holds the record for the fewest teeth of any bat.

Because the numbers of tooth types and the total number of teeth vary widely among bat species, teeth are often used as a key for identification. The greatest number of teeth found in any bat species is 38; this number occurs in many species worldwide. The jaws of insectivorous bats also differ among species, and like the teeth, reflect needs associated with their diet. For example, species that specialize in hard-bodied insects like beetles have strong jaws, whereas species that feed almost exclusively on moths and other soft-bodied insects have less powerful jaws.

Vision

The most widely held myth about bats is that they are blind. How this got started, no one knows for sure, but it may have originated in an area where the local bats roosted in caves. Because there is no light within caves, eyes are of no use and a number of cave-dwelling animals, such as blind cave fish and blind cave salamanders, no longer have eyes at all. It may have been assumed that since bats live in caves, they are blind as well. But, contrary to this popular myth, all bats have eyes and use them when light levels permit.

Because bats are nocturnal, their eyes are adapted for seeing in dim light. Like the eyes of most nocturnal animals, the lens is highly refractive, with a short focal length, providing a brighter image in low light, and the retina includes densely packed rods, increasing the amount of light collected per unit of area. During a laboratory experiment, it was noticed that a microchiropteran bat could distinguish between black-and-white patterns on a chart when the human observer could not even see the bat! While all bats tend to share these characteristics, there are other characteristics of the eyes that vary significantly, especially between megachiropteran and microchiropteran bats and, to a lesser extent, among bat families and genera. One obvious difference is that megabats have much larger eyes, both in absolute size and relative to the size of the body. Larger eyes, like larger cameras, provide larger images. Larger images on a larger retina allow greater visual resolution. This enables megabats to have higher visual acuity. Microbats have no pigmentation within the retina and therefore, like many mammals, see only in shades of gray. Most, but not all, megabats have some retinal pigmentation and can, to some extent, visualize color.

Another difference is that megabats have considerable binocular (3-D) vision, while microbats have little. To accomplish binocular vision, the left and right eyes must have overlapping fields of vision. The eyes of microbats are oriented more side-to-side, providing a minimal field of overlapping vision, while the eyes of megabats point nearly straight ahead, providing a much larger field of overlapping vision. Another factor affecting the ability of an animal to achieve three-dimensional sight is the connection of the neural pathways from the eyes to the brain. In microbats, as with most mammals, the retinal nerves from the right eye connect to the left brain (left superior colliculus), and the retinal nerves of the left eye connect to the right brain (right superior colliculus). In megabats, however, the retinal nerves from the right portion of each eye connect to the left superior colliculus, and the retinal nerves from the left portion of each eye connect to the right superior colliculus. As a result, the left and right superior colliculus in megabats each has visual information that can be compared and the differences used to create a three-dimensional mental picture. Prior to the mid-1980s, this visual pathway arrangement was known only in primates.

Reproduction

Like most mammals, female bats give birth to live young and produce milk to nourish them. There is, however, considerable variability in the reproductive cycles of the world's many bat species. Insectivorous bats in temperate zones have a unique reproductive cycle adapted to their climate. Since insects are

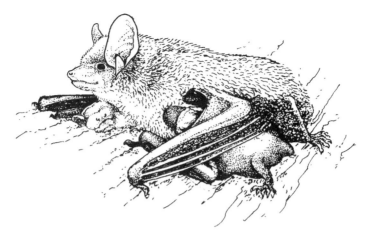

Figure 1.7. Female bat with pups.

scarce during the colder months in northern regions, bats begin to hibernate in the fall when temperatures drop. After a summer of foraging for insects, males are in peak physical and reproductive condition, making early fall the optimal time for mating. Unfortunately, it will soon be time for hibernation. Female bats work around this problem by storing the sperm in their reproductive tract during hibernation. In late winter or spring, as females arouse from hibernation, ovulation and fertilization take place. This delayed reproductive cycle enables the young to be born in late spring and early summer when insect availability is high. Most Florida species follow this pattern of mating in fall and giving birth in spring, even though few truly hibernate through the winter.

For their size, bats are considered the slowest reproducing of mammals. Female bats of most species have only one pup per year, although some have twins. The genus *Lasiurus*, of which we have four species in Florida, are unusual among bats because they can give birth to a litter of up to four pups. Temperate bats usually have only one reproductive cycle per year and it takes most young bats more than a year to become sexually mature and produce a second generation. Most other small mammals, such as mice and rats, can have litter sizes as high as a dozen and can produce young several times during a year that can become sexually mature within a few months. A single pair of rodents, for example, can produce thousands of offspring annually; however, a compensating factor is that their lifespans are short.

In Florida, most bat pups are born from late April through June after a gestation period of 45–90 days, depending on the species. Bat pups are relatively large at birth, usually weighing 20–30 percent of the mother's weight. They are generally born without fur and with their eyes closed. Their feet are almost adult size at birth because hanging on is critical for their survival. Some bats give birth by temporarily hanging in a head-up position so the pup drops into their tail membrane; others give birth in their normal head-down position, catching the young in their wing membrane. Like some other mammals, pups are born with milk teeth designed for hanging onto the mother's nipple. They acquire permanent teeth about the time they are ready to fly and forage on their own. During the early stages of growth, mothers leave their pups in the roost while they forage at night, but may return often at intervals to feed their young, which they recognize by individual pups' calls and scent.

Pups grow quickly. After a few weeks, they begin flapping and stretching their wings while clinging tightly to the roost surface with their feet. Many will take their first flight about three weeks after birth. Learning to fly, maneuver, and use echolocation well enough to catch insects in the night sky require agility and practice. While the pups, now referred to as juveniles, are practicing these skills, the mother bat is still lactating and providing milk to supplement their diet. By mid-August, young bats in Florida are sufficiently skilled in flight and capturing insects that they can forage on their own. In some cases, the birthing and rearing of young takes place in colonial roosts that are used year-round. In other cases, maternity colonies are formed at a specific location suitable for this purpose, and the colony breaks up or moves at the end of summer. For bats that do not form colonies the mothers and young simply go their separate ways. To a great extent, specific information is lacking and additional studies are needed to better understand what bats are doing following the maternity period.

Lifespan, Torpor, and Hibernation

For their size, microchiropteran bats are the longest-lived of the mammals. Researchers studying bats in northern states and Canada have documented bats with lifespans of more than thirty years. It is possible that temperate species in the northern portions of their range have longer lifespans because they spend much of the year in hibernation. A few bat species have been found hibernating in north Florida caves, but most bats at southern latitudes are active year-round. They can, however, enter torpor (a state of reduced metabolic activity) on cold or rainy nights when insect activity is low. While in torpor, bats lower their body temperature to within a few degrees of the surrounding air temperature. Their breathing, heart rate, and metabolic rate are all greatly reduced. This allows them to conserve energy until the temperature warms up and insects are available once again. Many temperate bat species use daily torpor as a means of conserving energy. Females will typically not use torpor during the latter part of gestation and while raising their young. Although bats can arouse themselves

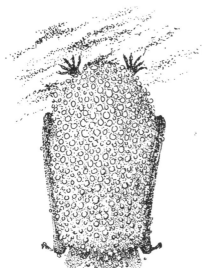

Figure 1.8. Hibernating eastern pipistrelle covered with moisture droplets.

from torpor at will, it takes a little time to return their heart rate and breathing to normal levels before they can sustain flight.

A frequent observation in this chapter has been the adaptations made by bats to accommodate flight. Bats serve as an example that great things are often accomplished only through great sacrifices. Bats will never walk upright like other mammals, but they have been masters of the night skies for more than 50 million years.

2

Natural History of Bats

Bats have been around for a very long time. The oldest bat fossil discovered has been dated at 53 million years. Bat fossils from this era of geological time, known as the Eocene, have been found in both North America and Europe. Scientists studying the fossils have determined that bats of the Eocene looked very much like the bats of today. Their skeletal structure shows they were fully flighted. Examination of fossil remains within the stomach reveals they were eating insects. Studies of their skulls and rib cages indicate they were echolocating. Given that the development of these characteristics would take some time to evolve, early bats likely shared the world with the last of the dinosaurs. It is remarkable, however, that bats have changed so little over the past 50 million years. They apparently found a unique niche in nature and developed the needed traits to exploit it; their ownership of the night skies has remained unchallenged for millennia.

The ancestry of these ancient bats, however, remains a mystery. No fossils have been found linking intermediate bats with their nonflying ancestors. Morphological studies, which analyze the physical makeup and structure of animals, tend to group bats with archontans (gliding lemurs, primates, and tree shrews). Molecular data, which is based on genetic studies, suggests bats should be grouped either with ferungulates (ungulates, whales, and carnivores) or eulipotyphlans (shrews, moles, and hedgehogs). Such a diversity of possibilities only serves to illustrate the large gap yet to be filled in our understanding of the evolution of bats.

Food Preferences

With so many species of bats in the world, it is not surprising they have developed a wide range of food preferences. There are insectivorous (insect-eating), frugivorous (fruit-eating), nectarivorous (nectar-feeding), carnivorous (meat-eating), and even sanguinivorous (blood-feeding) species. Fossil records indicate that ancient bats were eating insects more than 50 million years ago, and insects are still the primary food source for most bats today. About 71 percent of the world's bat species eat insects. All bats in the eastern United States eat in-

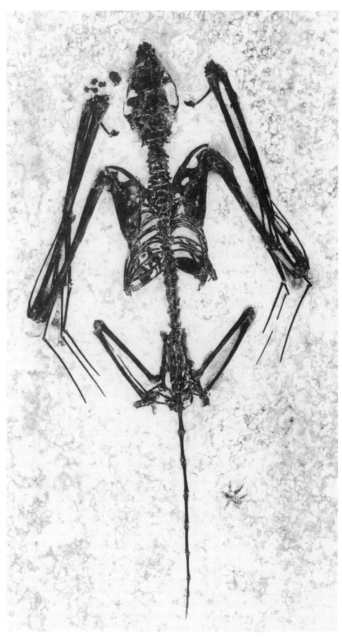

Figure 2.1. Bat fossil (*Icaronycteris index*) (copyright Peabody Museum of Natural History, Yale University, New Haven, Connecticut, USA).

Figure 2.2. Fishing bat using hind legs to gaff a small fish.

sects, with the exception of a few nectar- or fruit-eating species from Cuba and the Bahamas that occasionally show up in south Florida or the Florida Keys.

Frugivorous bats are found primarily in tropical regions of the world and feed on many fruits edible to humans such as figs, mangos, avocados, papayas, and bananas. They also feed on a number of items that humans would not consider edible, or even to be a fruit, such as flower petals and the pulpy outer layer of certain palm seeds. Most megachiropteran bats feed on fruit, but many also feed on nectar and pollen. There are a number of microchiropteran bats that eat fruit, nectar, and pollen as well. About 23 percent of the world's bat species are frugivorous and 5 percent are nectarivorous.

Less than one percent of bat species are carnivorous, but their diet includes a wide variety of prey. There are carnivorous bats that eat fish, frogs, lizards, birds, and small mammals (including other bats). Although the number of species is few, carnivorous bats are found in many areas of the world, including Mexico, Central and South America, Asia, Africa, and Australia. Fishing bats fly low over the water and use echolocation to detect ripples on the surface. They then reach down with their large hind feet and capture small fish swimming just beneath the surface. The bat stores the fish in cheek pouches until it can fly to a perch and eat it. Frog-eating bats in Central America listen to the calls of frogs and, based on their call, determine whether they are edible or poisonous.

Vampire bats, however, attract the most attention for their unusual food source. Only three of the more than 1,000 species of bats (0.3 percent) are sanguinivorous. They are found only in Central America, South America, and southern Mexico. Of the three species, the hairy-legged vampire (*Diphylla ecaudata*) feeds solely on the blood of birds, and the white-winged vampire (*Diaemus youngii*) feeds on the blood of birds and some mammals. The common vampire bat (*Desmodus rotundus*) feeds primarily on the blood of mammals and is the one most responsible for the fictional horror stories describing huge bats attacking innocent victims. As is often the case, real life is not so exciting. Common vampire bats are actually quite small, measuring only about 3½ inches (70–90mm) in length. Their main target today is livestock. Originally, their food source was limited to wild mammals, but with the influx of cattle ranching and farming in Central and South America, their food supply has been greatly expanded and their population has increased accordingly. Unfortunately, local farmers have tended to indiscriminately destroy all bat colonies, including many beneficial bats, while attempting to control vampire bat populations. Work is being done to educate farmers and ranchers on how to control vampire bat populations without destroying other valuable bat species in the process.

Bat Predators

One of the benefits of taking to the night skies is avoiding the numerous predators that feed on small animals. The strategy has worked well and, as a result, bats have a limited number of natural predators. Birds and snakes seem to be the only regular predators of bats, and seldom do bats make up a significant portion of their diet. Owls, being strong nocturnal hunters, prey on bats, and occasionally the skull of a bat will be found in an owl pellet. Birds of prey such as hawks, falcons, and kestrels will occasionally linger near a bat roost at emergence time and capture one or more bats as they leave the roost. The darkening sky, however, limits the window of time available to these predators, since their hunting depends on daytime vision. In Florida, various species of snakes will find their way into a roost and prey on sleeping bats. A number of other animals will also eat a bat if the occasion arises. These might be referred to as "opportunistic" predators. In Florida, this list would include animals such as raccoons, opossums, blue jays, and crows. An introduced predator that must now be added to this list is the domestic cat.

Roosting Behaviors

An animal is most vulnerable to predators when it is sleeping. One approach to solving this problem is to find a good hiding place; another is to develop some sort of camouflage. Bats use a little of both. With respect to roosting behaviors, bats can be divided into two groups: colonial bats and solitary bats.

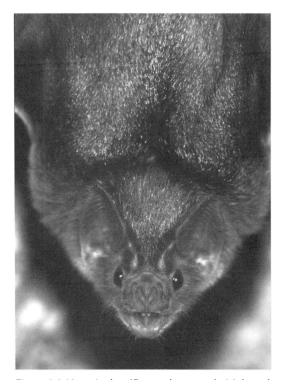

Figure 2.3. Vampire bat (*Desmodus rotundus*) (photo by Barry Mansell).

Colonial bats, as their name implies, roost in groups. The size of bat colonies varies among species and with roost site availability, but can range from just a few bats to thousands, and in some cases, millions of bats. The colony of Brazilian free-tailed bats that occupies Bracken Cave in Texas during the summers has been estimated to number more than 22 million. This is the largest single grouping of mammals found anywhere in the world. Colonial roost sites need to be secure, so bats choose such things as caves, tree hollows, and crevices. It is difficult for a predator to reach a bat hanging from the ceiling of a cave, or for a bird to reach back into a small crevice.

Bats that do not form colonies are referred to as solitary bats. Although some solitary bats roost in caves, most roost in trees. Occasionally, more than one solitary bat will be found roosting in the same tree, but they are not roosting together or in groups. In Florida, solitary bats often hide within clusters of dead palm fronds or within clumps of Spanish moss. Because they are more exposed, solitary bats depend more heavily on camouflage. The yellowish tan color of the northern yellow bat, for example, blends in so well with dead palm fronds that one is easily missed even when looking directly at it. The slight grayish tint of an eastern pipistrelle can render it virtually invisible within a clump of Spanish moss. The frosted, multicolored fur of the hoary bat provides excellent

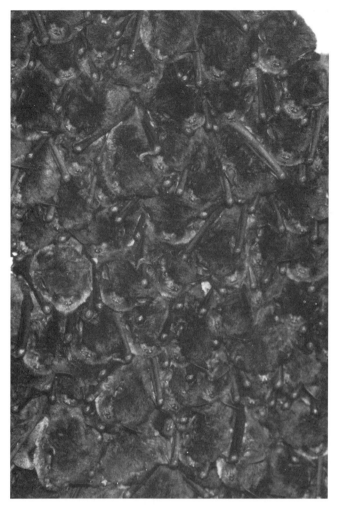

Figure 2.4. Colony of southeastern myotis roosting in cave (photo by Barry Mansell).

camouflage in a variety of roosts. Because solitary bats do not have the benefit of shared warmth from roosting partners, they tend to have longer and thicker fur.

Other factors influencing the selection of roost sites include protection from the elements, the temperature of the roost, distance to water and foraging areas, and during the maternity season, suitability for rearing young. Some roosts may satisfy all of these needs all year long, and bat colonies will adopt them permanently. Others may meet the needs of a colony only at certain times of the year. In these cases, bats will move from one roost to another on a seasonal basis. For example, some colonies may have both a summer and a winter roost. Once roosts are found that meet the needed requirements, bats become very loyal to them, either remaining permanently or returning year after year. Manmade structures can also provide the needed requirements, and some species of bats

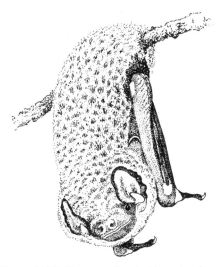

Figure 2.5. Solitary roosting bat hanging from a twig.

will readily inhabit them. Bridges, attics, eaves, and roofs often become roost sites for colonies of bats. Unfortunately, in many cases, the bats are unwelcome and fearful home and building owners frequently destroy entire colonies of bats. This has become so important to bat conservation that chapter 7 is devoted solely to this topic.

Migration

At first it was assumed that bats did not migrate, but banding studies quickly revealed that some bats migrate hundreds of miles. This was surprising considering that flight is very energy intensive for bats. It was also surprising because northern bats could simply go into hibernation to avoid the winter cold and would have no apparent need to migrate. Understanding what would drive bats to migrate helps unravel the mystery. An obvious reason is the avoidance of stressful climatic conditions. Bats avoid roost sites with freezing temperatures. Below freezing, even hibernation can be energy expensive. Colonial bats overcome this by finding suitable cave roosts with temperatures above freezing. Tree-roosting bats, however, do not have this option and must find a location with suitable temperatures. Another factor that drives animals to migrate is the seasonal abundance of food resources. Airborne insect activity is at a minimum during the winter in colder climates. This can be addressed through winter hibernation or migration to warmer climates. But even hibernating bats may migrate from a cave or mine shaft after winter to a summer foraging area and then return the following winter. A third factor is the need to find a location to birth and rear young, an activity that requires a suitable roost site and abundant food resources. This last reason is of foremost importance to female bats and it has been found that female bats are more likely to migrate, and often migrate longer distances than males. Although a few bat species may migrate a thousand miles or more, most bat migrations are in the range of a few hundred miles.

Many bat species, however, do not migrate and some individuals and groups of individuals within migrating species do not migrate. For example, Brazilian free-tailed bats migrate long distances between the southwestern United States and Mexico, but in Florida, California, and western Arizona, this species does not migrate. Among nonmigratory bats, some use the same roost year-round, but others may move seasonally from one roost to another within the same general vicinity. These movements are driven primarily by the need to find roost sites with desirable temperatures as the seasons change, and by females seeking suitable roosts to birth and rear young. Because of their short distances (usually less than 100 miles) and because they are within the same climatic region, these movements are not defined as migratory.

Little is known about the cues used by bats for migratory navigation. Some evidence suggests they may be using visual information. Echolocation would be of little use because of its short range. Studies on certain bird species indicate they may be using the earth's magnetic field for orientation, but similar studies have not yet been conducted with bats. Occasionally, bats have been observed migrating at night along with birds; whether this is to take advantage of the birds' aptitude for long-distance navigation or for other reasons is yet unknown.

Benefits of Bats

Many people seem to feel that for an animal to be worth conserving, it must be of some benefit to humans. This is a somewhat self-centered point of view, though not uncharacteristic of humans. It should be sufficient that an animal has been an inhabitant of the planet for millions of years, and consequently has an inherent right of its own to remain present. Fortunately for bats, they are beneficial to humans in a number of ways, giving us something to work with in justifying their conservation.

Insect Control

Most of the world's bats are insectivorous and, subsequently, insect control is a major benefit of bats. This is certainly true in Florida. All of our resident bat species are insectivorous. When we think of insect control, the first insects that come to mind are mosquitoes. Although some bats are known to eat mosquitoes, mosquitoes may constitute only a small part of the diet of Florida bats. Nonetheless, we will take all the help we can get. In addition to eating mosquitoes, Florida bats play a role in controlling many other nuisance insects.

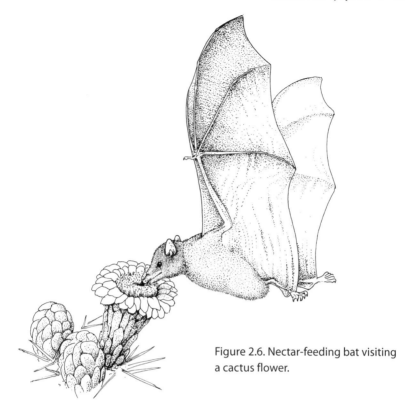

Figure 2.6. Nectar-feeding bat visiting a cactus flower.

Included in the diets of Florida bats are moths, beetles, flies, midges, flying ants, swarming termites, leafhoppers, mosquitoes, caddisflies, true bugs, and more. Bats around the world have proven to be a major factor in the natural control of a number of agricultural pests. For example, Brazilian free-tailed bats out west are known to be a major predator of the corn earworm moth (*Helicoverpa zea*). This agricultural pest, also known as the cotton bollworm and tomato fruit-worm, is considered the number one agricultural pest in North America. It attacks sweet corn, tomatoes, soybeans, cotton, and a variety of other agricultural plants. More work needs to be done to determine the quantities and species of insects being eaten by Florida bats. Bats could be playing a significant role in the control of agricultural pests in Florida, as well.

Pollination

Nectar-feeding bats are important for the pollination of many valuable plants such as wild banana, agave, date, balsa, and kapok. Worldwide, there are more than 500 plant species pollinated by bats. In some cases, plants and bats have evolved together to the point that the plant can be naturally pollinated only by bats. In those cases, if the bat populations were to decrease or disappear, so would the plants. In the southwestern United States, there are three species of nectarivorous bats (*Choeronycteris mexicana*, *Leptonycteris curasoae*, and *Leptonycteris nivalis*) that pollinate important desert plants such as saguaro and organ pipe cacti, as well as agaves. These bats winter in Mexico and migrate northward in the early spring to take advantage of the cacti blooming in the desert regions of the southwestern United States. One of the agaves pollinated by these bats is used to make tequila, a famous liquor of Mexico. The flowers of some agaves open only at night in anticipation of the fleeting visits of foraging bats. There are no resident nectarivorous bats in Florida, but occasionally a species common to the Caribbean will show up in southern Florida.

Seed Dispersal

Bats are vital to the rapid reforestation of cleared rainforests. Fruit-eating bats digest their food rapidly and deposit seeds with their droppings as they fly. This behavior distributes seeds over a wide geographical area. Studies have shown that seeds from bat droppings germinate faster and have a higher survival rate, benefiting from the digestive process.

Fertilizer

Bat guano has been mined for centuries throughout the world as a high-quality fertilizer. In many countries it still remains an important natural resource. Once chemical fertilizers became readily available in developed countries, the use of bat guano for fertilizer dropped off. Bat guano is high in nitrogen, phosphorus, and potassium. It is water soluble, making it ideal for hydroponic gardening. It contains living microbes, enabling it to also serve as a soil builder, soil cleanser, and compost activator. Many organic gardeners today choose bat guano for fertilizing vegetables, fruit trees, and ornamental gardening. During the 1800s, numerous caves around the world were damaged, and bat colonies impacted, to facilitate the mining of bat guano in large quantities. Fortunately, as the result of increased environmental awareness, most large cave-mining operations are now conducted with minimal additional cave damage, and in ways that do not interfere with bat colonies.

Gun Powder

Bat guano became of strategic importance during the American Civil War, when it was discovered to contain saltpeter, the main ingredient in gunpowder. During the war, tons of bat guano were mined from caves throughout the United

States and used by both the Union and the Confederacy. In fact, bat guano was used for the production of gunpowder as late as World War I. Kilns used for drying bat guano can still be seen at the mouth of Frio Cave in Texas.

Medical Research

The common vampire bat, famous for its role in horror films, is also famous in the medical world for its saliva. When a vampire bat bites its victim, it slices the surface of the skin with its sharp incisor teeth and laps up about two tablespoons of blood from the wound. While licking the wound, an enzyme in the bat's saliva temporarily prevents the blood from clotting. This unique enzyme, formally known as "Desmodus rotundus salivary plasminogen activator" (DSPA), or more simply as Desmoteplase, is more than a hundred times more powerful than previously known blood clot–dissolving drugs. Desmoteplase uniquely attacks only the blood clots themselves and does not affect the balance of the clotting system. This characteristic greatly reduces the risk of intracranial bleeding and consequential brain damage. Because of this, DSPA can be administered up to nine hours after a stroke, enabling many more patients to receive treatment and thereby reducing the number of stroke victims suffering from paralysis, speech disorders, and disabilities. Real-life vampire bats may actually save more lives than their fictional cousins were credited for killing in those late night horror movies!

Sound Navigational Ranging (SONAR)

Even bat echolocation has benefited humans. In 2002, researchers at Britain's Leeds University announced they had used bat echolocation as a model for what they have called the "batcane." The batcane enables people who are visually impaired to detect objects beyond the reach of the conventional white cane. The batcane issues high-pitched sounds inaudible to the human ear. When the electronics in the cane detect an echo from an obstacle in front of the user, it triggers a vibration in one of four pads on the cane's handle. As an object is approached, the speed of the vibration increases. The pads alert the user of the presence of obstacles to the left, to the right, forward at head height, and forward at ground level, giving the user a mental image of what lies ahead. Because the cane communicates through touch, the user does not need to rely on hearing, and is free to carry on a conversation or listen for other sounds. This new device was marketed by Sound Foresight, Ltd., beginning in 2004, as the "UltraCane." Early reports from users indicate they felt much more comfortable with the new UltraCane than the conventional white cane and freer to go out on their own.

～

It is amazing that prejudices, myths, and misunderstandings within our society can cause so many people to consider bats frightening and repulsive. As we learn more about bats, their unique characteristics, their place in the balance of nature, and their benefits to humans, we can only hope it will help us to more easily recognize and overcome other prejudices and misconceptions as well.

3

Echolocation

How bats are able to navigate in total darkness had been a mystery for centuries. In the late 1700s, a few studies were conducted to determine how bats were accomplishing this feat, but they led to what was then considered a preposterous conclusion: bats were somehow using their ears to "see in the dark." Of course, everyone "knew" this was ridiculous, so the studies were considered flawed; after some ridicule and scoffing they were filed away and forgotten. It was not until the late 1930s that the mystery was solved. The generally accepted theory up until that time was that bats detected the returning air currents off obstacles with their wings.

After the sinking of the Titanic in 1912, thought was given to developing a means of preventing such disasters in the future. Sir Hiram S. Maxim, well-known in his time as an engineer and inventor, proposed a system that would generate powerful low-frequency sounds, with listening devices to detect the returning echoes. He based this idea on his thinking that bats might be feeling the reflections of low-frequency sound waves created by their wingbeats. The proposed device was never built, but it was the first time sound was suggested as the possible medium for bat navigation. Though it might work for ships, the wavelength of low-frequency sounds would be so long that bats would only be able to detect objects larger than 50 feet in width. Later, in 1920, an English physiologist, H. Hartridge, proposed that perhaps bats were using high-frequency sounds to avoid objects while in flight. No work, however, was performed to test the theory. One of the confounding factors was that although bats make audible sounds while in their roosts, most species make no audible sounds while in flight.

The mystery was finally solved by Donald R. Griffin, a young Harvard undergraduate student, who at the time was banding bats to study their migrations. Griffin was familiar with the supposition that bats felt air currents reflected from obstacles with their wings and Hartridge's proposal that bats might be using high-frequency sounds for navigational purposes. In 1938 he was informed by a friend that George W. Pierce, a physics professor at the university, had developed an apparatus that could detect sounds above the human hearing range. At the time, such sounds were referred to as "supersonic," but that term was

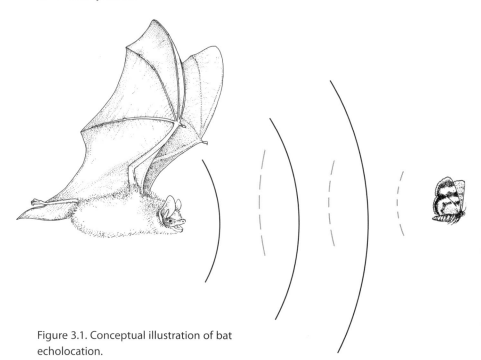

Figure 3.1. Conceptual illustration of bat echolocation.

later relegated to high-speed aircraft, and the term used today is "ultrasonic" sounds. With some trepidation, Griffin approached Professor Pierce and asked if it would be possible to use his device to listen to bats. The professor agreed, and shortly thereafter, Griffin carried a cage of bats up to the professor's laboratory. When he first held the cage in front of the large parabolic microphone, both he and the professor were surprised and delighted to hear, as Griffin put it, "a medley of raucous noises from the loudspeaker." The bats were obviously making ultrasonic sounds, but the question remained, were they using them for navigational purposes? Griffin embarked on a series of studies that proved bats were, in fact, navigating using high-frequency sounds, and he named the process "echolocation."

Echolocation in the Animal Kingdom

Upon further study, it was discovered that the echolocation capabilities of microchiropteran bats are nothing short of amazing. From the returning echoes, microbats can determine how far away an object is, its size, shape, texture, whether it is approaching or receding, and how fast it is moving. Microbat echolocation can even detect something as fine as a human hair. Scientists have strung thin wires from floor to ceiling only 12 inches apart and bats with 11-inch wingspans are able to fly between them with ease in total darkness. Most megabats, on the other hand, do not have echolocation capabilities. Like other nocturnal animals, they use their eyes and depend on the moon and stars as a source of light. There are, however, exceptions. Two cave-roosting species have developed a rudimentary form of echolocation for navigating the dark interior of caves. The Egyptian rousette bat (*Rousettus aegyptiacus*) clicks its tongue on the roof of its mouth to generate a sound and listens for the returning echoes. Geoffroy's rousette bat (*R. amplexicaudatus*) utters a high-pitched buzzing sound.

Experiments conducted in the 1950s suggested that dolphins might also be using echolocation, but it was not until 1960 that it was scientifically proven that dolphins, like bats, were navigating through the use of echolocation. Dolphin echolocation is as sophisticated as that of bats, but has a few advantages, such as higher speed and longer range, because water provides a better medium for transmitting sounds than air. Other toothed whales also use echolocation, and certain species of shrews, tenrecs, and rodents echolocate to varying degrees. Among birds, there is a cave-dwelling bird known as the oil bird, or guácharo, in Trinidad and South America, and several species of cave-dwelling swiftlets in Southeast Asia, that echolocate.

A more sophisticated term used for echolocation in the animal kingdom is "biosonar." The word comes from the naval acronym SONAR, which stands for Sound Navigation and Ranging. Sonar, as the name implies, uses generated sounds and returning echoes to detect objects, and is applied primarily underwater. It became a household word during World War II when it was used for detecting mines and submarines beneath the ocean's surface.

RADAR, which stands for Radio Detecting and Ranging, is based on the same principle as sonar, but uses electromagnetic waves rather than sound waves. Radar works well for monitoring aircraft and weather because electromagnetic waves are not appreciably attenuated in the atmosphere; it therefore has a much greater range. Because it was discovered that bat echolocation is extremely accurate and that bats gain considerable information from the returning echoes, the military has often studied bats to learn more about their echolocation capabilities.

Making Loud Sounds

The first step in echolocation is to make a loud sound. Bats generate echolocation calls using their lungs and larynx, just as we do when we talk, sing, or shout. Everyone knows if you want to hear a good echo, you need to yell out loudly. Likewise, if a bat is going to hear an echo off a moth or mosquito, it

Table 3.1. Sample Vocalization and Hearing Ranges

Vocalization/Emission	Low (Hz)	High (Hz)
Human	85	1,100
Piano	30	4,100
Songbird	2,000	13,000
Dog whistle	12,000	15,000
Bat echolocation[a]	9,000	200,000
Tiger moth	20,000	120,000

Hearing Ranges	Low (Hz)	High (Hz)
Human	20	20,000
Dog	15	50,000
Cat	60	65,000
Bat[a]	1,000	200,000
Moth	20,000	60,000

a. The echolocation and hearing ranges of bats vary significantly from species to species. The ranges given here encompass all species worldwide.

also needs to yell loudly. Bats with high intensity (loud) calls yell out at 110–120 decibels (db). Decibels are a way of measuring the loudness of sounds. A 110 db sound is about as loud as a household smoke detector held four inches from your ear. If our ears could hear bat echolocation calls at that distance, it would be painful, but fortunately or unfortunately, depending on your point of view, we cannot hear them.

A frequently used term in describing bat echolocation calls is hertz (Hz), which by definition is one cycle (vibration) per second. A thousand cycles per second is referred to as a kilohertz (kHz). Table 3.1 lists the frequencies of a few selected sounds and hearing ranges as examples. Children with excellent ears can hear sounds as high as 20 kHz. Upper hearing levels drop off with age, so adults seldom hear that high. Sounds above the human hearing range of 20 kHz are referred to as "ultrasonic" sounds. As can be seen from figure 3.2, most Florida bat species echolocate within a range of 20–70 kHz. There is one Florida species, the Florida bonneted bat, with search calls in the 10–16 kHz range. These calls are well within the human hearing range and can be heard by most people with good ears. Another Florida bat, Rafinesque's big-eared bat, echolocates at up to 90 kHz. There are bats elsewhere in the world that echolocate at frequencies of more than 100 kHz.

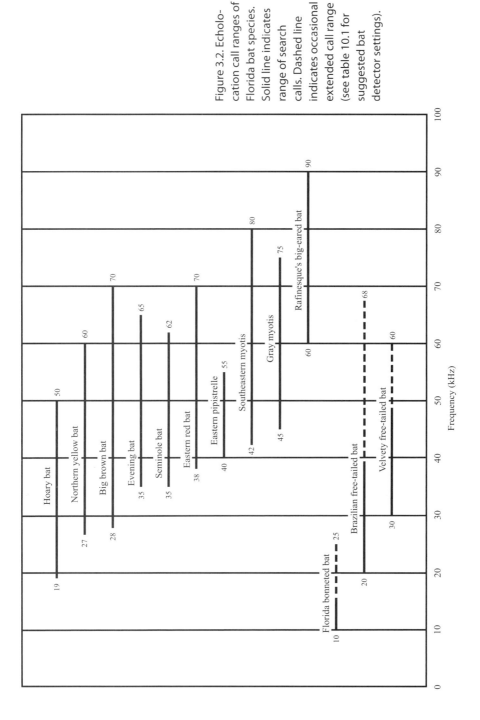

Figure 3.2. Echolocation call ranges of Florida bat species. Solid line indicates range of search calls. Dashed line indicates occasional extended call range (see table 10.1 for suggested bat detector settings).

Seeing with Echoes

When bats are navigating with echolocation, they usually issue their echoloca-tion calls as a series of individual yells or chirps at a rate of 10–20 per second. A series of such calls is often referred to as a "call sequence." The sound from each chirp creates echoes as it bounces off objects in its path. During the short space of time between each call, the bat listens for returning echoes. Even though the echoes are brief and faint, they provide a lot of information. The length of time it takes for an echo to return indicates how far away an object is. If several echoes return, the earliest ones indicate the closest objects. Another indicator is the strength of the returning echoes. When coupled with timing, louder echoes indicate larger or harder (more reflective) objects.

Another important factor is the frequency (pitch) of the returning echo. Some bats use the Doppler effect to gain information regarding the movement of objects. The Doppler effect refers to the fact that sound waves (and radio and light waves as well) are compressed by an approaching source, resulting in a higher frequency, and stretched out by a receding source, resulting in a lower frequency. This is why the sound of a passing truck makes a changing high- to low-pitched roar as it passes by while you are standing alongside a highway. The change in pitch can be used to determine if the object is approaching or receding, and how fast it is moving. Although the primary benefit is to discern the movement of prey relative to the bat, some bats also use this phenomenon to determine the type of insect they are targeting. You may have noticed that different insects have different wing flutter patterns. As the echolocation calls bounce back from the insect's wings, the changing positions of the wings modu-late the pitch of the returning echoes. Bats soon learn the wing flutter patterns of insects that make good meals.

Using Echolocation to Capture Insects

The original quest by scientists was to determine if bats were using echolocation for navigational purposes, but it was soon discovered that bats were using it also to capture insects in the night skies. The study of bat foraging behaviors and the application of their echolocation skills to the challenging task of capturing insects in midair have proven to be an interesting field of study that continues to provide amazing discoveries. Most insectivorous bats begin foraging by flying a relatively linear course, while calling out about 10–20 echolocation calls per second. These fairly uniform and evenly spaced calls are referred to as "search calls." This portion of the bats' maneuvers is likewise referred to as the "search phase." Search calls are issued in synchrony with the bat's wingbeats. Just as it is easier for you to breathe in while you raise your arms and exhale as you lower them, the bat issues its echolocation calls on a wingbeat downstroke with little or no extra effort. Consequently, very loud calls can be made by expending little additional energy.

Depending on a number of factors, such as size of the insect, humidity of the air, and intensity of the call, bats can detect an insect about 10–15 feet away. Once an echo is heard returning from an insect, the bat changes its flight path and swoops toward the insect. At this point, the insect will likely attempt to escape. The bat now needs more information to track its evasive prey. More information requires more echoes, so the bat doubles or triples its call rate. Some bats also change the pitch and bandwidth of their calls to expand the type of information received via the echoes. These "approach calls" indicate the bat is now pursuing the insect and is in the "approach phase" of its attack.

Now the bat will attempt to capture the insect in midair. Think of how difficult it is to catch a flying insect with your hand. Imagine doing it by shouting at it and listening to echoes! The insect at this point exercises extreme evasive measures, and the bat needs even more rapid and more accurate information. The attacking bat will issue up to 200 calls per second and interpret 200 echoes per second. The calls are so rapid that on bat sonar detecting equipment (bat detectors) it sounds like a buzz, and is referred to as the "feeding buzz." This portion of the bat's maneuvers is called the "capture phase." When the feeding buzz is heard, one can see the bat do a dive, loop, or turn as it captures the insect. The bat may catch the insect in its mouth, in its wing, or in its tail membrane. It devours the insect while in flight, then once again begins to issue search calls. This process is repeated hundreds of times per hour as the bat forages during the night. Bats do not always successfully capture the insect because, as we shall see later, insects have developed a few tricks of their own.

Detecting Ultrasonic Sounds

Because humans cannot hear bat echolocation calls, we need help if we are to study them. Bat detectors have been designed to detect the echolocation calls of bats and produce corresponding sounds at audible levels. There are three basic types of bat detectors: heterodyne, frequency division, and time expansion. *Heterodyne bat detectors* are based on the same principle used to tune radios and televisions to specific stations. The difference is, however, that radio and television tuners are designed to work with electromagnetic waves and bat detectors are designed to work with sound waves. Essentially, this process filters out all sounds except the ones selected on the tuning dial. *Frequency division bat detectors* divide the frequency of the detected sound by a constant number to transpose it from the ultrasonic range to the audible range. For example, a 40 kHz sound divided by 10 results in a 4 kHz sound, which is easily within the audible range. The main advantage of the frequency division design is that it converts the full spectrum of detected sound frequencies to the audible range, whereas the heterodyne bat detector makes audible only that portion of the sound (frequency range) permitted to pass through the filtering process. *Time expansion bat detectors* capture the sound and slow it down, causing it to be both reduced in frequency and expanded in time. This would be like recording a sound at full speed on a tape recorder, then playing it back at a slower speed. All three approaches are helpful in studying bat echolocation calls. The use of heterodyne bat detectors is discussed further under "Bat Watching with a Bat Detector" in chapter 10. Because frequency division and time expansion bat detectors transpose the full spectrum of sounds detected, they are the types of detectors used to analyze bat echolocation calls.

Analyzing Bat Echolocation Calls

Sound waves are essentially vibrations within the air. They are three-dimensional and complex. To understand sound waves, we must use simplified representations. One of these is a two-dimensional representation of the sound pulse. In this view, as shown in the upper portion of figure 3.3, time is represented on the horizontal axis, and amplitude, or intensity, is represented on the vertical axis. In this example, it can be seen that the intensity is greater toward the end of the pulse. Frequency is represented by the number of times per second the waveform crosses zero. The more crossings per second, the higher the frequency, but this is difficult to see in the sound pulse representation.

Another way of representing the same sound is to plot the frequency with respect to time. This is called a sonogram and is shown in the lower portion of figure 3.3. You can now see that the sound begins at a higher frequency (pitch) and ends at a lower one. The intensity of the sound with respect to time may be represented by varying either the thickness or color of the line. Sonograms have proven to be very useful in the study of bat echolocation calls. The characteristics of the sample pulse and associated sonogram shown here are typical of many vespertilionid bat calls.

Just as bird calls can be used to identify birds, bat calls can be used to identify bats. It is more difficult to identify bat calls because we cannot hear them directly and must depend on electronic equipment for analysis. Technology, however, has risen to the occasion, and by coupling computers with bat detectors, we can now plot sonograms directly (in real-time) as the bat flies overhead. With time expansion devices, we can hear the bat call in slow motion, so to

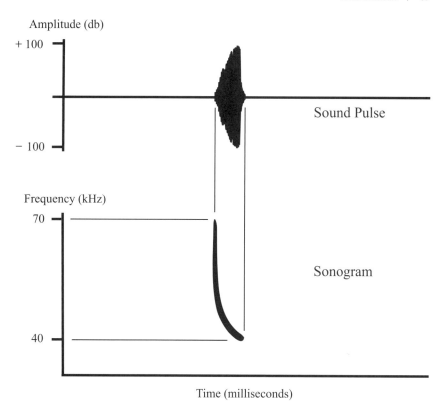

Figure 3.3. Sound pulse of a typical vespertilionid bat echolocation call (top) and associated sonogram (bottom).

speak. Tools like these enable a field worker to both analyze a call sequence as it comes in and store it as a computer file for future study. Details regarding the methods for identifying species from sonograms and identifying Florida bats in particular would justify a book in itself. We will focus here on the concepts and describe a few Florida bat calls for comparative purposes. Figure 3.4 will serve as the basis for the following discussion and illustrates the search calls for two Florida bat species. Bats may vary their calls significantly to navigate in cluttered areas or to approach and capture insects. Consequently, search calls in open areas have proven to be the most useful for species identification, since they tend to be more consistent and unique. When sonograms of bat calls are plotted, the silent period between calls is often omitted to enable more calls to be shown on a chart. For example, on the charts shown here, there may be only a few milliseconds (ms) shown between calls, when actually the space between calls may have been 50–100 milliseconds.

Frequency (kHz)

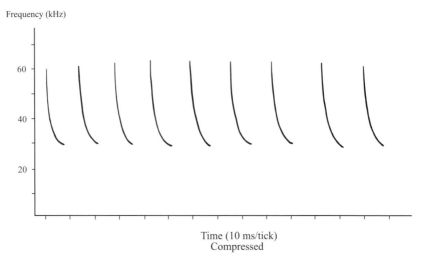

Time (10 ms/tick)
Compressed

Figure 3.4a. Search calls of a big brown bat.

Frequency (kHz)

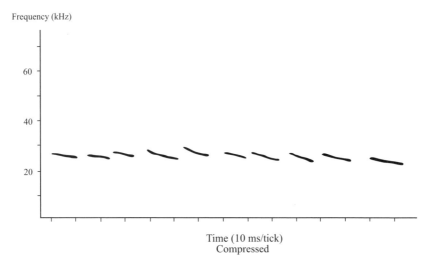

Time (10 ms/tick)
Compressed

Figure 3.4b. Search calls of a Brazilian free-tailed bat.

Figure 3.4a is a series of echolocation calls from the call sequence of a big brown bat. These calls cover a broad range of frequencies (broad bandwidth), beginning at 60 kHz and dropping to 30 kHz. Figure 3.4b shows a series of calls from the call sequence of a Brazilian free-tailed bat. When you compare these, notice that the frequencies of the Brazilian free-tailed bat calls are much lower, ranging from about 28 kHz to 24 kHz in this example. Also, the free-tailed bat

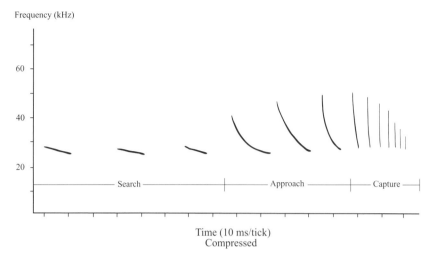

Figure 3.5. Echolocation call sequence of a Brazilian free-tailed bat.

calls are nearly linear with a slight downward slope, rather than tall and curved. The calls cover a much narrower band of frequencies (narrow bandwidth), with each call spanning less than 5 kHz. Although it is easy to see the differences in the calls of these two bats, there are many vespertilionid bats with tall curved calls and many molossid bats with downward sloped linear calls. In fact, identifying bats by their calls is seldom easy. For example, bats change their calls as they approach insects or fly within cluttered areas, such as near tree foliage. Also, the top portions of the calls are often lost because higher frequencies are attenuated more rapidly in the atmosphere. In particular, differentiating species within the same genus can be a challenge. In such cases, it often requires careful analysis of a number of call characteristics to make a positive identification.

By using bat detectors, it is possible to trace a full sequence of echolocation calls, ranging from search to capture. Figure 3.5 illustrates the call sequence of an attacking Brazilian free-tailed bat. Notice that as the bat approaches the insect, it increases the rapidity, pitch, and bandwidth of its calls. This increases the speed and accuracy with which information is gathered as the bat pursues the fleeing insect. In light of the bat's high-tech insect-tracking capabilities, one might wonder if insects have any chance of escaping.

Insect Responses

As might be expected, insects have developed a few tactical measures of their own. Many insects have developed the ability to hear. Some moths, crickets, katydids, and lacewings have a pair of ears and can determine the direction of an approaching bat. Mantids, on the other hand, have only a single ear, and although they can detect an approaching bat, they cannot determine its direction. Insect ears detect sounds in the 20–60 kHz range, which encompasses the frequency spectrum of most echolocating bats. Because some of these insects have no way of making noises, it is felt that their ears are used solely for the detection of bats. Others, however, use sounds to attract mates, so their ears may serve a dual purpose. Studies show that having ears reduces an insect's chance of being captured by as much as 40 percent.

For an insect, the first step in avoiding a bat attack is to determine the magnitude of the threat. Some insects determine how far away a bat is by the loudness of the calls, but others use the rate at which the calls are issued. Because bats homing in on insects increase their call rates, insects can use this information to help determine the appropriate tactical measures. Upon detecting the search calls of bats, the early-avoidance strategy for most insects is to move out of the area. If, however, they hear the increased call rate of a bat in the approach phase, they begin exercising more extreme measures, such as dives, loops, and turns. Some moths immediately fold their wings and drop three to four feet to escape the bat. In a variation of this tactic, lacewings fold their wings, drop, and then suddenly open them again, as air brakes. The bat, having more inertia, speeds by and misses. The disadvantaged praying mantis, having only one ear, and therefore not able to determine the direction of the approaching bat, enters a steep power dive. Unlike the drop of moths and lacewings, the mantis uses its wings to dive straight down at twice its normal flight speed. Obviously, if you don't know where the bat is coming from, the safest direction is down.

Arctiid moths, also known as tiger moths, have developed an even more sophisticated means of defense. Located on the surface of the moth near the ear are tymbal organs made up of a series of grooves in the chitin (the hard material that forms the exoskeleton). This area can be flexed or buckled by muscular tension, causing a series of high frequency clicks that closely resemble bat echolocation calls. When these moths detect a bat in pursuit, they buckle the area, issuing a series of ultrasonic sounds.

At first it was thought these sounds were to either startle the bat or interfere with its reception of the echoes. Later studies, however, revealed that once bats have tasted a tiger moth they prefer never to eat one again. While in the caterpillar phase, tiger moths eat plants that are toxic, and these toxins are passed on to the adult moth, causing it to have a really bad taste. In fact, bats have even been seen spitting them out!

It is now believed that the noises made by the arctiid moth are actually a signal notifying the approaching bat to pass them by or suffer the consequences.

Insects with bad tastes have initiated this same defense strategy with birds by adopting very bright colors rather than camouflage. Colors, however, are not of much use at night, so this appears to be an acoustical form of what is called "aposematism" (a method of warning predators of a defense mechanism).

Bat Countermeasures

If insects have developed defenses, you might expect that bats have developed countermeasures, and so they have. Bat countermeasures consist of stealth, stealth, and more stealth. Echolocation is an active and noisy process. Most insect ears can detect a bat call when it is more than 100 feet away, long before the bat can hear the returning echoes. On the opposite end of the spectrum, ordinary hearing is a passive process; that is, one listens quietly to surrounding sounds. The advantage of passive hearing is that the listener does not reveal its presence or position. Some bats stop echolocating and use sounds made by their prey to locate them, even though they could have accomplished it through echolocation. In such cases, the echolocation calls may have been discontinued to prevent alerting the insect. A related approach is to reduce the intensity of the calls. Some bats issue echolocation calls in the 60–80 decibel range. This is about the intensity of someone whispering in your ear, and consequently, these bats are often referred to as "whispering bats." Bats with low-intensity calls may be homing in on the sounds made by the insect, and using echolocation only to keep track of the background environment for navigational purposes. The call intensity is such that the insect does not hear the bat until it is only a few feet away and has little time left for escape. Both strategies tend to be used by gleaning bats, those that pick up insects from foliage or the ground. Gleaning bats fly slowly and can more readily accept the shortened acoustical range of lower intensity calls.

A different strategy adopted by bats is to echolocate at frequencies either above or below the hearing range of insect ears. Some bats echolocate at more than 100 kHz, well above the range of insect ears. Taking an opposite approach, there are a few bat species that echolocate in the audible range, which is well below the hearing range of insect ears. Sacrifices are made, however, on both counts. High-frequency sounds are rapidly attenuated in the atmosphere, so high-frequency bats have a much shorter echolocation range. Low-frequency sounds, on the other hand, have long wavelengths, and the returning echoes provide less detail and accuracy with respect to small targets.

The reluctance of early scientists to accept the results of detailed studies suggesting that bats were using their ears to navigate in total darkness demonstrates how preconceptions can prevent us from accepting new ideas. The development of bat echolocation, insect ears, moth noise generators, insect avoidance tactics, and bat countermeasures illustrates the complex interrelationship of adaptations that can evolve over millennia, as species struggle for survival. A war has been raging in the night skies for millions of years, but we were not aware of it until 1938 when Donald R. Griffin (1915–2003) began his pioneering work in bat echolocation.

4

Bats in Florida

Florida emerged from the seas a little more than 25 million years ago during a period known as the late Oligocene. Prior to that, its entire geological history had been under water. This makes Florida a rather young landmass by geological standards. During these relatively few years (geologically speaking), sea levels rose and fell by hundreds of feet on numerous occasions, creating multiple seashores and landmass configurations. Florida has fluctuated from a fraction of its current size to twice its current size. This, coupled with associated climatological shifts, resulted in constantly changing ecosystems within Florida. As time passed, Florida's climate ranged from tropical to semiarid, and its ecosystems included, in varying proportions, moist forests, deciduous forests, pine forests, mixed hardwood forests, grassy woodland savannas, and sandhill scrub. The present swamps, bay heads, and lakes were a later addition, occurring within the last several thousand years. All of this, however, would be less daunting to bats than to their terrestrially bound mammalian cousins. Bats could readily expand or contract their range to match this changing environment. It is not surprising that Florida's early fossil records include five families of bats: the Emballonuridae (sheath-tailed bats), the Mormoopidae (mustached bats), the Natalidae (funnel-eared bats), the Phyllostomidae (leaf-nosed bats), and the Vespertilionidae (plain-nosed bats). Bats continued to appear in Florida's fossil record, although families and species emerged and disappeared. Fossil records indicate that vampire bats (family Phyllostomidae) once even flew over Alachua, Marion, and Citrus counties: *Desmodus archaeodaptes* during the early Pleistocene, and *Desmodus magnus* during the late Pleistocene (18,000 years before present). This rich and diverse history has led to the present-day flora and fauna of Florida, including the current array of bat species. Even today, the presence and range of various species continues to change. Most changes are due to the intrusion and expanding range of humans, but forecasts suggest that a warming climate and rising sea levels may also once again impact Florida.

Table 4.1. Occurrence of Bat Species by Region in Florida

Name	Northwest	North	Central	South	Keys
Resident Species					
Big brown bat (*Eptesicus fuscus*)	U	U	R	R	—
Brazilian free-tailed bat (*Tadarida brasiliensis*)	C	C	C	C	—
Eastern pipistrelle (*Pipistrellus subflavus*)	U	U	U	U	—
Eastern red bat (*Lasiurus borealis*)	C	C	U	—	—
Evening bat (*Nycticeius humeralis*)	C	C	C	C	—
Florida bonneted bat (*Eumops floridanus*)	—	—	—	R	—
Gray myotis (*Myotis grisescens*)	R	—	—	—	—
Hoary bat (*Lasiurus cinereus*)	R	R	—	—	—
Northern yellow bat (*Lasiurus intermedius*)	C	C	C	C	—
Rafinesque's big-eared bat (*Corynorhinus rafinesquii*)	U	U	R	R	—
Seminole bat (*Lasiurus seminolus*)	C	C	C	U	—
Southeastern myotis (*Myotis austroriparius*)	C	C	U	—	—
Velvety free-tailed bat (*Molossus molossus*)	—	—	—	—	U
Northern Accidental Species					
Indiana myotis (*Myotis sodalis*)	A	—	—	—	—
Northern long-eared myotis (*Myotis septentrionalis*)	A	—	—	—	—
Silver-haired bat (*Lasionycteris noctivagans*)	A	—	—	—	A
Southern Accidental Species					
Buffy flower bat (*Erophylla sezekorni*)	—	—	—	A	A
Cuban flower bat (*Phyllonycteris poeyi*)	—	—	—	—	A
Jamaican fruit-eating bat (*Artibeus jamaicensis*)	—	—	—	—	A
Cuban fig-eating bat (*Phyllops falcatus*)	—	—	—	—	A

Note: C = Common, U = Uncommon, R = Rare, A = Accidental, — = Not expected or never recorded.

Florida Bat Species

Twenty species of bats have been recorded in Florida. Thirteen are classified as resident and seven as accidental. They are members of three families: the Vespertilionidae, the Molossidae, and the Phyllostomidae. Twelve of the resident species give birth and rear their young in Florida, and are found here year-round. Whether the hoary bat resides in Florida year-round remains in question. To date, it has been confirmed to be in Florida only from October through April; however, there are unconfirmed reports of its presence during the summer. The hoary bat, known to be highly migratory, was once thought to migrate through Florida from the north to an unknown winter range in the south, but records are suggesting it is more likely expanding its range from northern states into Florida during the cooler months of the year. The eastern red bat is also known to be migratory, and although found year-round in Florida, its

NORTH

NORTHWEST

CENTRAL

SOUTH

FLORIDA KEYS

Figure 4.1. Definition of the regions in table 4.1 used to describe range differences of bat species in Florida.

abundance varies seasonally. Species classified as accidental are those for which occasional (rare) specimens are found, but for which there is no evidence that the species is living in the area or returning on a regular basis. Of the accidental species, three are of the family Vespertilionidae and four are from a more tropical family, the Phyllostomidae.

The ranges of bat species in Florida appear to be driven by climate, availability of roost sites, and abundance of food sources. Florida spans more than six degrees of latitude, and the climate ranges from temperate in the north to subtropical in the south. North Florida experiences occasional freezes, but the likelihood of freezing temperatures drops off significantly as one moves south. The central and southern portions of the state are bounded on either side by water, elevating the humidity and causing a summer season of convectional rains. This progression of higher temperatures, higher humidity, and increased rainfall impacts both the flora and the fauna as one progresses from north to south. The ranges of bat species in Florida often become a question of how far south a temperate species will range or how far north a tropical species will range.

Table 4.1 lists the bats of Florida, identifying species as either resident or accidental. The regions listed in the tabulation are illustrated in figure 4.1 and designed to best describe the relative abundance and range differences of Florida bats. The table also indicates the regions in which accidental species have been found. More detailed information and range maps are provided for each species in chapter 5.

Occurrence of Accidental Species in Florida

Florida's geographic location makes it susceptible to accidental species. Because north Florida borders the continental United States and the southern portion dips toward the Caribbean basin, Florida has two distinctively different sources of accidental species. We refer to species arriving in Florida from the north as "northern accidentals" and species arriving from the south as "southern accidentals." The following is a general discussion of accidental species occurring in Florida. Chapter 5 contains more information on each species and the specimens recorded. Table 4.1 lists the accidental species in Florida and classifies them as northern or southern accidentals. Appendix C summarizes the accidental specimens recorded in Florida.

With respect to the northern portion of the state, a unique geographical feature enhancing the possibility of accidentals from the north is the system of rivers flowing through Georgia and Alabama into Florida. Although the Apalachicola River lies totally within the state of Florida, it is formed by the confluence of the Flint and Chattahoochee Rivers at Lake Seminole. The headwaters of the Flint River are just south of Atlanta, and the headwaters of the Chattahoochee River are in north Georgia, just south of the North Carolina border. This river system provides a natural corridor funneling temperate biota to the south. In particular, the Apalachicola River bluffs and ravines are noted for containing temperate hardwood tree species that are disjunct from their normal range in the Appalachian Mountains. Caves in this area also appear to meet the requirements of these temperate bat species, and the area is the southern extent of the established range for the gray myotis, a resident species. Some maps also show it as the southern extent of the range for two northern accidentals: the Indiana myotis (two specimens recorded) and the northern long-eared myotis (one specimen recorded).

The third species classified as a northern accidental is the silver-haired bat. One specimen was found in Santa Rosa County near the Alabama border (about 100 miles south of its known range). Another was found in Bahia Honda State Park in the Florida Keys. The known roosting behaviors of this bat lead to speculation that this individual may have been brought into Florida on a

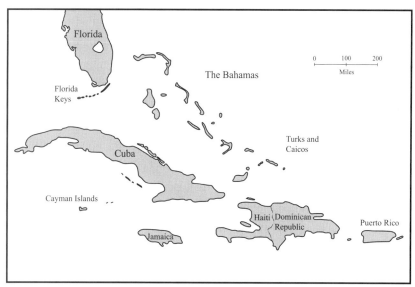

Figure 4.2. Map of the Greater Antilles showing proximity of Florida to Cuba and the Bahamas.

recreational vehicle (RV). Bahia Honda State Park is a popular RV camping destination.

In the past, the little brown myotis (*Myotis lucifugus*) was listed as a species occurring in Florida, on the basis of several Florida specimens. The southeastern myotis (*Myotis austroriparius*), a common species in north Florida, and the little brown myotis, a species with a more northerly range, can be difficult to distinguish based on external features alone. Because of past errors in the identification of these two species, the Florida specimens have been re-examined and all were found to be the southeastern myotis. Consequently, the little brown myotis is not included as occurring in Florida.

The southern portion of the state, on the other hand, borders the Caribbean. The east coast of Florida is within 70 miles of the Bahamas, and the southern tip of the Florida Keys is within 90 miles of Cuba. Bat species native to the Caribbean have occasionally made an appearance in south Florida. To date, four phyllostomid species have been found and are classified as southern accidentals: the Jamaican fruit-eating bat, the buffy flower bat, the Cuban flower bat, and most recently, the Cuban fig-eating bat. Bats fitting the description of the family Phyllostomidae have also been seen on several occasions and even photographed, but specimens were not collected, so their identity is either unknown or in question. Searches for roosts and colonies so far have not confirmed that any of these are permanently or seasonally living in Florida. As a result, these species remain classified as accidental, but it is not impossible that one or more could become established in the area. The history and status of bats in the Florida Keys is unique and discussed in more depth later in this chapter.

Another factor likely to promote accidental species is continued traffic across Florida borders. Transportation by land, sea, and air provides uncountable opportunities for introduction of nonnative species into Florida. Bats have occasionally been found under rolled-up awnings of motor homes and campers, and clinging to sailboat rigging. Some of the specimens currently listed as accidentals may have arrived in this manner. At one time, both megachiropteran and microchiropteran fruit bats were imported and sold in the pet trade, but the practice was made illegal in 1995. To date there is no known bat species established in Florida as a result of this practice, but illegal importation of bats is still a matter of concern.

Natural Roost Habitat in Florida

Natural roost sites in Florida consist primarily of tree foliage, tree cavities, Spanish moss, palm fronds, and caves. Table 4.2 summarizes the common, naturally occurring bat roost sites in Florida. The category labeled "Tree Foliage" consists of the leaves, branches, twigs, and leaf stems of hardwood trees. The roost habitat labeled as "Tree Cavities" includes tree hollows, woodpecker cavities, cracks caused by splits, loose bark, and any cavity or crevice caused by insects or decay. This category includes both living and dead trees. The column labeled "Spanish Moss," as the name implies, refers to the use of Spanish moss (*Tillandsia usneoides*) as a roost site. The category labeled "Palm Fronds" includes both live fronds and dead palm thatches hanging below the live fronds. The palm most used by bats in Florida is the cabbage palm (*Sabal palmetto*), also referred to as the sabal palm. Washingtonia palms, imported from Mexico (*Washingtonia robusta*) and California (*Washingtonia filifera*), have even thicker and longer thatches of dead fronds running down much of the trunk and are known also to serve as bat roosts. A few Florida bat species have occasionally been found using royal palms (*Roystonia* spp.) as a roost site. In these cases, colonies have been found near the base of the palm leaf stem where it meets the trunk. The column labeled "Caves" refers to natural Florida limestone caves.

Table 4.2 differs from data presented in more general texts on the bats of North America, since this table specifically indicates the habitat that bat species use as roost sites in Florida. For some species, the roosting habitat selected in Florida is different from elsewhere in their range. More detailed information on the roosting behaviors of each species is provided in chapter 5.

Table 4.2. Naturally Occurring Roost Sites Commonly Used by Bats in Florida

Name	Tree Foliage	Tree Cavities	Spanish Moss	Palm Fronds	Florida Caves
Family Vespertilionidae					
Big brown bat	—	F	—	R	—
Eastern pipistrelle	F	O	F	—	F
Eastern red bat	F	—	R	—	—
Evening bat	—	F	R	—	—
Gray myotis	—	—	—	—	F
Hoary bat	F	O	R	—	—
Northern yellow bat	—	—	F	F	—
Rafinesque's big-eared bat	—	O	—	—	R
Seminole bat	F	—	F	—	—
Southeastern myotis	—	O	—	—	F
Family Molossidae					
Brazilian free-tailed bat	—	R	—	R	—
Florida bonneted bat	—	O	—	R	—
Velvety free-tailed bat	—	—	—	—	—

Note: F = Frequently, O = Occasionally, R = Rarely, — = Not expected or never recorded.

Cave Habitat in Florida

The Florida peninsula is essentially a limestone plateau. It was created over millions of years while Florida was submerged under warm, shallow seas. Over the millennia, sea creatures lived and died in these warm waters, sinking to the bottom at the end of their lives and accumulating on the sea floor. Florida limestone bedrock, the foundation of the Florida peninsula, is made up of their fossilized and calcified remains. Florida limestone is soft, soluble, and rich with the fossils of these ancient sea creatures. After Florida rose above sea level, rainfall and surface water seeped through cracks and crevices in the limestone, dissolving the bedrock and making it porous. Holes and openings enlarged with time, allowing water to accumulate and flow within the thick limestone layer. These underground streams and rivers continued to erode the bedrock and eventually formed the caves and sinkholes typical of the Florida karst (eroded limestone) region. Although the karst region covers much of north and central Florida, there are only two areas (figure 4.4) that contain caves suitable as bat roosts. Florida caves differ from caves found to the north. They are warmer, have a higher humidity, are walled with soft limestone or dirt, and have less expansive interiors.

Three Florida resident bat species are considered cave-roosting bats: the southeastern myotis, the gray myotis, and the eastern pipistrelle. Two of the species listed as accidentals were found roosting in Florida caves: the Indiana myotis and the northern long-eared myotis. Three other Florida resident spe-

Figure 4.3. A cave entrance in north Florida (photo by Jeff Gore/FWC).

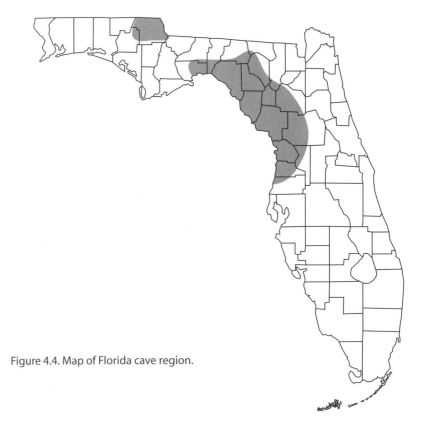

Figure 4.4. Map of Florida cave region.

cies that normally roost in caves elsewhere have rarely or never been found roosting in Florida caves: Rafinesque's big-eared bat, the big brown bat and the Brazilian free-tailed bat. This may be because of differences in the temperature, humidity, size, or roosting surfaces of Florida caves. For some, it may be the lack of a need to hibernate. An unfortunate hazard related to Florida caves is that some are subject to flooding. Flooding caused by tropical storm Alberto in 1994 trapped a colony of southeastern myotis in the domed area of a cave in northwest Florida, drowning an estimated quarter-million bats. Cave-dwelling bats are also susceptible to disturbance and vandalism. A simple careless or purposeful act can destroy an entire colony consisting of thousands of bats. The protection of Florida caves is discussed in chapter 6.

Impact of Manmade Structures

Humans have been living in Florida for more than 10,000 years. Early Florida inhabitants were nomadic hunters of mammoths, bison, camels, and giant tortoises—and may have contributed to the extinction of this megafauna. As these larger animals disappeared, they resorted to smaller game, shellfish, fish, and plants. About 800 years ago, they turned to agriculture, and at that point began to have an impact on the landscape. Their impact was minor, however, compared to the influx of European colonists that began in 1763, when Florida was ceded by Spain to England. Much has been said about the loss of natural habitat as growth and development progressed in Florida. Certainly, loss of natural habitat has had a major impact on Florida bats, just as it has on nearly all of Florida's natural flora and fauna. Agriculture and urban development have replaced much of Florida's hardwood forest, pine flatwoods, and sabal palm hammock. During the peak of the Florida logging industry, most of the old growth longleaf pine and bald cypress forest were harvested. The collection of Spanish moss for stuffing furniture and automobile seats removed literally tons of bat habitat, and likely, thousands of bats were destroyed in the process. Fortunately, the impact of these latter two industries on bats has waned with time, as natural resources have become more precious and alternative materials have been developed. However, logging continues on a smaller scale, and Spanish moss is collected today as a medium for arts and crafts and gardening.

There is yet another, perhaps unexpected, impact of urban expansion in Florida that uniquely affects bats: the introduction of manmade structures. As habitats were destroyed, buildings were erected in their place. For tree-dwelling species unable to adapt to manmade structures, this meant a net loss of habitat, and they were squeezed out of urban areas as development progressed. For other bat species, buildings and manmade structures provided alternative

Table 4.3. Species Known to Use Manmade Structures in Florida

Name	Buildings	Bridges	Culverts	Utility Poles	Bat Houses
Family Vespertilionidae					
Big brown bat	F	O	R	—	O
Eastern pipistrelle	O	—	—	—	—
Evening bat	F	F	—	F	F
Rafinesque's big-eared bat	F	R	R	—	R
Southeastern myotis	O	F	F	—	O
Family Molossidae					
Brazilian free-tailed bat	F	F	—	—	F
Florida bonneted bat	F	—	—	—	O
Velvety free-tailed bat	F	—	—	[a]	[a]

Note: F = Frequently, O = Occasionally, R = Rarely, — = Not expected or never recorded.
a. Although velvety free-tailed bats have not yet been found roosting in utility poles or bat houses in Florida, their roosting habits elsewhere within their range suggest they would likely use these structures.

roost sites. Some species appear to prefer them and have all but abandoned their natural roost habitat. Of Florida's resident species, the Brazilian free-tailed bat, big brown bat, evening bat, Florida bonneted bat, southeastern myotis, and Rafinesque's big-eared bat are frequently found in manmade structures (table 4.3). Brazilian free-tailed bats, which appear in Florida's fossil records as early as the late Pleistocene, have essentially abandoned natural roost sites in favor of manmade structures. This observation was made during a survey conducted by William L. Jennings in the 1950s, and continues to hold true today. The velvety free-tailed bat, a late entrant onto the Florida scene, has been found roosting only in manmade structures. Although few roost sites for the Florida bonneted bat have been located, information so far indicates they may prefer manmade structures as well, making this a tendency of molossid species in Florida. The proliferation of manmade structures may be facilitating the range expansion of these bats and increasing their abundance. Of course, all of this good news doesn't come without a downside and that is that most people don't want bats in their buildings. To protect and conserve bats in Florida, we must address the use of manmade structures by bats. This topic will be discussed more fully in chapters 6 and 7.

Bats in Florida also use a number of other manmade structures, as shown in table 4.3. Bridges rank second to buildings as potential bat roost sites. More than 400 bridges serve as bat roosts in Florida. Culverts are used by southeastern myotis, but it is rare to find other bats using them. Utility poles also serve as bat roosts, but are used almost exclusively by evening bats. They roost behind the brackets that support such things as transformers, street lights, capacitors,

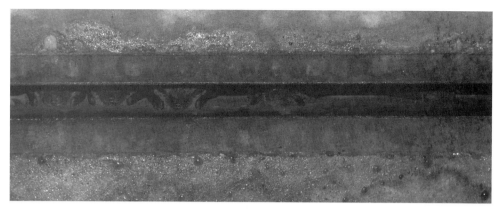

Figure 4.5. Big brown bats roosting in a bridge crevice (photo by George Marks).

and electrical switches. Bat houses provide roosting habitat for six of the eight Florida species that will move into manmade structures. Chapter 8 is dedicated to the design and location of bat houses in Florida. There are also various other manmade structures that can serve as roost sites that are not listed in table 4.3. Basically, any structure with small crevices or gaps can potentially be adopted by bats as a roost site.

Bats in the Florida Keys

Bats were first reported in the Florida Keys by C. J. Maynard in 1870, while cataloging the mammals of Florida. He had seen large bats flying over Key West and collected a specimen that he identified as *Artibeus perspiccilalune,* an old scientific name for the Jamaican fruit-eating bat, but the identification was later disputed. Bats were also noted during the 1920s, when Clyde Perky built a bat tower for mosquito control on Sugarloaf Key. His superintendent, Fred Johnson, said they knew bats were present because they had been found roosting in telephone junction boxes (chapter 8). The intriguing part of this story, however, is that when Jennings conducted his survey of Florida bats in the 1950s, he found no bats in the Florida Keys. The following is a quote from his final report, "The ecological distribution of bats in Florida" (1958, pp. 39–40):

> The Florida Keys, which offer migrating birds a welcome pathway leading to the tropics, apparently do not function in this way for bats. None were collected or reported from the area during the study despite an intensive search. More than 20 residents, bird watchers, nurserymen, pest control specialists, and others were contacted, some of them repeatedly, over a period of three years. Transects were run in the town of Key West and

at a large borrow pit filled with brackish water on Big Pine Key, the two localities which seemed to represent the most attractive habitat for bats. No bats were observed.

This is interesting, given the earlier reports and the current status of bats in the Keys today. Were the bats reported by Maynard a chance occurrence? What species of bats were getting into the telephone junction boxes? Why were they not there in the 1950s? At that time, it was generally felt there was an insufficient supply of fruit and flowering plants in the Florida Keys to support a population of frugivorous bats and insufficient fresh water to support insectivorous bats. It is likely the bats in the telephone junction boxes were insectivorous, since that type of roost matches their known preferences. Whatever the species, they were not found in the 1950s when Jennings conducted his survey. Fred Johnson also stated that, contrary to widespread rumors, Perky did not import bats for his bat tower. This leads us to conclude that the current population of velvety free-tailed bats now found in the Florida Keys was not imported by Clyde Perky, nor were they present in the 1950s. The first colonies were discovered in the mid-1990s in buildings on Boca Chica Key, Key Vaca (Marathon), and Stock Island. Over the following years, colonies were found in various locations throughout the Lower Keys. Some of these colonies have now disappeared or have been excluded from their building roosts. In 2004, a colony was discovered in the Upper Keys in a building on Plantation Key, which represents a significant expansion of their range but does not necessarily indicate an overall increase in their abundance. At present, this is the only bat known to be established in the Florida Keys.

During the 1970s and 1980s, there were other scattered sightings of what people referred to as "large bats" in the Lower Keys, but no specimens were collected. Then, in the 1990s and early 2000s, isolated specimens of phyllos-tomid bats were found and recorded. The collected species were identified as the Jamaican fruit-eating bat, the buffy flower bat, the Cuban flower bat, and the Cuban fig-eating bat. To date, repeated attempts to locate colonies or viable populations of these bats have failed, and these species remain classified as accidentals.

The question of whether or not Neotropical fruit- or nectar-feeding bats could colonize the Florida Keys remains open. Given that the climate of the Lower Keys is reasonably similar to that of their native environment, two other requirements need to be met for colonization: food resources and roosting habitat suitable for reproduction. Previous to human colonization, most of the Florida Keys were simply rocky outcroppings with mangroves and sparse vegetation. There was little or no standing fresh water. Such a landscape would likely be uninhabitable by both insectivorous and frugivorous bats. The mas-

Figure 4.6. Postcard of Florida Overseas Highway in 1927 (courtesy of Monroe County Public Library).

sive immigration of humans, beginning in the late 1920s, changed all of this. Buildings, bridges, towers, utility poles, ponds, and swimming pools abound. For species that are able to adapt to manmade structures, roost sites are now available on nearly every major key. Water is imported via a pipeline from the mainland, and landowners have successfully planted innumerable exotic fruit trees and flowering plants, including mango, banana, avocado, sapodilla, ficus, breadfruit, and palms. It is possible there now exists a year-round supply of fruit, flowers, nectar, and pollen for bats. With respect to habitat, the Jamaican fruit-eating bat, in its native environment, roosts in caves, hollow trees, rock crevices, and manmade structures. The Cuban fig-eating bat frequently roosts in tree foliage, primarily that of mahogany trees, which is a native tree of south Florida. It would appear these two species could be likely candidates. The buffy flower bat and the Cuban flower bat are both cave-dwelling species, making them less-likely candidates. In order to survive in the Keys, they would need to adopt alternate forms of roosting habitat. The Cuban flower bat would appear to be the least-likely candidate because of its specific requirement for hot caves with high humidity.

∼

The dynamic aspects of bat behavior, colonization, and range expansion in Florida provide exciting material for biologists and bat enthusiasts. Why have molossid species essentially abandoned their natural roosts in Florida? Why have certain cave-dwelling species living in Florida not adopted Florida caves as roosts? How far north will velvety free-tailed bats range? Why have Brazilian free-tailed bats not moved into the Keys? Will they at some future date? If so, how will the two species interact? Will other Neotropical bat species appear in south Florida? Will frugivorous or nectarivorous bats establish viable populations in south Florida? What will be their impact, if any?

5

Florida Bat Species

This chapter presents a description of each of the bat species found in Florida. Descriptions are arranged first by family, then alphabetically by scientific name. This approach groups species by family and genus, making it easier to recognize similarities and differences. The index can be used to find species by their common names.

Measurements are provided for body length, total length, wingspan, forearm length, and weight. Most measurement parameters are self-explanatory, but a few comments are in order. Body length is measured from the tip of the nose to the base of the tail and does not include any part of the tail or tail membrane. Total length is measured from the tip of the nose to the tip of the tail. In tailless bats it is measured to the last caudal vertebra. Wingspan is the distance from wingtip to wingtip. Wingspan may be helpful in gaining a mental picture of the size of a bat's silhouette in flight. While the bat is roosting, the wings are folded up against the side of the body, and usually only the forearms are visible. The forearm length is measured from the outside of the wrist to the outside of the elbow. It is an important parameter when identifying bat species.

The measurements provided are not from a specific set of samples, but are a generalization based on reference material and measurements made by the authors. Metric values are given for all measurements; however, typical values for wingspan, total length, and tail length are also provided in English units for those who do not have a feel for metric measures. Forearm measurements are given solely in metric since they would be used only for species identification, which use is based on metric units. Weights are not given in ounces since, in nearly all cases, the weight would be expressed as a fraction of an ounce, and would not be very useful in gaining a feeling for the weight of a species. For those who do not normally use metric weights, it may be helpful to note that a dime weighs just over two grams.

The range maps in this chapter provide the current distribution in Florida for each species. They were constructed on the basis of a review of reference material combined with the personal experience of the authors. Shaded areas on the maps indicate the regions in Florida where the species is known or reasonably expected to be found. Three levels of shading are used. The darkest shading indicates areas where a species is abundant. The medium level of shading indicates areas where a species is uncommon. The lightest level of shading indicates areas where a species occurrence is rare. In the case of accidental species, a dot indicates the locations where specimens were found; details of these are included in the text and summarized in appendix C.

Including a section on bats in the family Phyllostomidae is relatively new for Florida. The Jamaican fruit-eating bat (*Artibeus jamaicensis*) was first confirmed in Florida when two specimens were found in Key West, one in 1995 and one in 1996. Both individuals were emaciated and died shortly after collection. The buffy flower bat (*Erophylla sezekorni*) was first documented when a dead specimen was found washed up on a beach in the Marquesas (west of Key West) in 1996. A live specimen was found in Miami in 2004. The Cuban flower bat (*Phyllonycteris poeyi*) was documented as being present when two dead specimens were found, one in Key West in 2001 and one on Stock Island (east of Key West) in 2002. A Cuban fig-eating bat (*Phyllops falcatus*) was discovered on Stock Island in 2004. Because of Florida's proximity to Cuba and the Bahamas, each with a large number of bat species, it is quite possible that other Neotropical species will appear in Florida from time to time.

Many bat species are similar in color and appearance. Because of this, bats are best identified by unique features and, in some cases, the careful measurement of those features. An illustrated identification key for Florida's resident species is provided in appendix D. Each step of the key provides a choice between two alternatives. Each choice leads either to another set of alternatives or to a species name, indicating an identification has been reached. Working through a key to identify a bat often requires restraining the bat in order to take measurements. Therefore, the identification key is intended for use by biologists and others who normally work with wildlife, and have rabies pre-exposure vaccinations. For some species, an identification may be possible by working through the key while closely observing, but not handling a bat.

The key is designed for identifying adult bats. In summer, volant juveniles may have the characteristics of an adult and may be identifiable by using the key, but their measurements will be slightly smaller and they are often darker in color. During this time, juveniles can be differentiated from adults by their uncalcified finger joints. The joints of juveniles are cartilaginous, and appear elongated and slightly translucent. By late summer, the finger joints have calcified and juveniles at this stage of development will essentially have the same measurements as adults. Also helpful when identifying a bat is knowing which species are expected to be in the geographical area. This can be determined by consulting the range maps in the species accounts and the summary of ranges in table 4.1. Once an identification has been made using the key, the species account should be consulted for more details regarding the distinguishing characteristics of that species.

Family Vespertilionidae

The family Vespertilionidae is the largest and most widespread of the bat families. It includes more than 40 genera and more than 350 species. Vespertilionid bats are found on all continents except Antarctica. The family name comes from the word "vesper," an old word referring to the evening, and provides an appropriate name for this family, since most vespertilionid bats emerge early in the evening. Occasionally, the family is referred to as the "vesper" bats. Vespertilionid bats lack the strange and unusual facial features found in some bat families and hence are also often referred to as "plain-faced" or "plain-nosed" bats. Most species have normally shaped ears, but a few have very long ears. Typically, vespertilionid bats have small eyes and a tail enclosed in a tail membrane. Nearly all species of this family are insectivorous; however, there are a few that feed on fish. Some species within this family are colonial and others are solitary. Some are migratory. Some hibernate during winter months. Vespertilionid bats have become an integral part of ecosystems around the world by adopting a wide variety of habitats and roost sites, and developing a diversity of feeding strategies.

Corynorhinus rafinesquii

Rafinesque's Big-eared Bat

Description. Rafinesque's big-eared bat is a medium-sized bat easily identified by its enormous ears, which measure 27–37 mm in length (about one inch). It has two large facial glands on its muzzle, bordering the nostrils. Because of this, it has occasionally been called the eastern lump-nosed bat. Its long, silky fur is grayish brown and distinctly bicolored, with individual hairs dark at the base and lighter at the tip. Dorsally, the hair tips are gray, while ventrally they

	Measurements	Categories
Wingspan:	260–300 mm (11 inches)	Family: Vespertilionidae
Body length:	38–56 mm (2 inches)	Florida occurrence: Resident
Total length:	80–110 mm (3¾ inches)	Florida status: Uncommon
Forearm length:	39–46 mm	Roosting behavior: Colonial
Weight:	7–13 g	Regional classification: Temperate

are white. Long toe hairs, which extend past the tips of the claws, are another distinguishing feature of this species (Plate 1).

Roosting behavior. Rafinesque's big-eared bats normally inhabit forested areas. In Florida, they have been found in pine flatwoods and hardwood hammocks. Although tree hollows and crevices behind loose bark are considered common natural roosting sites for this species, they are more often found roosting in unoccupied or seldom used buildings. In Florida, they have been found in abandoned trailers, sheds, hunting cabins, and similar structures, particularly in wooded areas. They usually enter through an open window or door and roost in semi-lit areas of an interior room.

Although cave use by this species is rare in Florida, in more northern states, Rafinesque's big-eared bats hibernate in caves, mines, and similar structures such as cisterns and wells. They are considered colonial and have been known to roost in groups of up to a hundred individuals, but they are more often found roosting in small groups, in pairs, or alone.

Foraging behavior. Rafinesque's big-eared bats begin foraging later in the evening than most Florida species, emerging from their roosts well after dark. Moths constitute the majority of their diet, but they feed on other soft-bodied insects as well. Rafinesque's big-eared bats are the only bats in Florida that use gleaning as one of their primary foraging strategies, but they also capture insects in the air. The broad wings and low wing loadings of these bats provide the needed maneuverability for a gleaning strategy. Observers have been amazed as they watch big-eared bats fly slowly between and around objects, and hover in place for several seconds at a time.

Reproduction. In the northern portion of their range, Rafinesque's big-eared bats are known to mate in the fall and winter. In Florida, there is some evidence that they may also mate during spring. Females give birth to a single pup in May or early June. Young bats begin to fly at about three weeks of age and reach adult size shortly after one month.

Range. Rafinesque's big-eared bats are found within the forested regions of the southeastern United States from the extreme eastern edge of Texas northward to southern portions of Illinois, Indiana, Kentucky, Ohio, West Virginia, and Virginia. In Florida, they have been found in scattered locations, mainly in the panhandle and the northern half of the peninsula. In 1992, an adult

Uncommon
Rare

female was found roosting in a log cabin in the Big Cypress Swamp region of northeastern Collier County. This finding may suggest that these bats were once more widespread throughout the state. It is also likely they were more abundant, and that their populations may have severely declined as a result of logging and development. These bats are so rarely encountered in Florida that little is known about their abundance and population trends.

Remarks. As hunting shacks, trailers, and other structures appeared in forested areas, this species found them attractive as roost sites, and moved in. When encountered by building owners or trespassers the bats are often intentionally killed. Structures like these are also used as maternity roosts. Because of their slow reproduction rate, the death of more than a few, and certainly the destruction of a maternity colony, could have a severe impact. Abandoned buildings in forested areas should be carefully checked for the presence of this bat before being moved or destroyed. The future conservation of the big-eared bat may depend on people who live in and around forested areas and allow them to roost undisturbed.

Eptesicus fuscus

Big Brown Bat

Description. The big brown bat, as its name implies, is a relatively large brown bat. Its fur is long and silky and varies in color from dark chocolate brown to reddish brown or golden brown. The fur on the underside is paler. The ears and flight membranes are dark brown or nearly black. The big brown bat has a relatively large head with a broad, dark, unfurred muzzle. The ears are small and dark, with a broad, rounded tragus. The calcar is keeled. The big brown bat is similar in appearance to the evening bat but can be identified by its larger size. A measurement of the adult forearm will easily distinguish it from the evening bat (Plate 2).

Roosting behavior. Tree cavities provide natural roosting habitat for this species, but today they are more often found in manmade structures. In buildings, they are typically found in attics, eaves, and behind shutters or decorative fascia. Other structures used for roosting include bridges, barns, picnic shelters, and

	Measurements	Categories
Wingspan:	320–350 mm (13 inches)	Family: Vespertilionidae
Body length:	53–81 mm (2½ inches)	Florida occurrence: Resident
Total length:	87–138 mm (4½ inches)	Florida status: Uncommon
Forearm length:	41–52 mm	Roosting behavior: Colonial
Weight:	11–23 g	Regional classification: Temperate

bat houses. In south Florida, a group of 18 females was found roosting in the base of a leaf stem of a royal palm. It is not known whether royal palms are regularly used or whether this was an unusual occurrence. Big brown bats have, on occasion, been found roosting with colonies of Brazilian free-tailed bats.

In the northern United States and Canada, big brown bats usually migrate short distances to a cave or abandoned mine where they hibernate through the winter, although they have occasionally been found hibernating in buildings. In Florida, this hardy species likely forages on all but the coldest nights of the year.

Foraging behavior. Big brown bats have strong jaws and heavy teeth, allowing them to feed on hard-bodied insects. Beetles make up a large portion of their diet, but they are also known to feed on planthoppers, true bugs, flies, mosquitoes, and other insects, including termites and carpenter ants during their flying stages. Moths, which make up a large portion of the diet of many bat species, are only a small part of the big brown bat's diet.

The big brown bat flies a fairly straight and steady course, veering off to capture insects. After an initial feeding period of 30–60 minutes when insect activity is high, big brown bats often rest at a night roost near the feeding area. Typical night roosts include sheltered areas such as porches, open garages, barns, and picnic shelters.

Reproduction. Big brown bats mate in the autumn and winter. Females store sperm until spring, when ovulation and fertilization occur. As with most species, timing of the birth of young varies with latitude. Although there is little information on the timing of births in Florida, it most likely occurs from May through mid-June, as with many other Florida species. Female big brown bats in the eastern United States typically give birth to twins, after a gestation period of about two months. In western states, females typically give birth to a single pup.

Range. Big brown bats are found throughout most of North America, ranging from southern Canada and Alaska through the United States, and southward through Mexico into northern South America. They are also found on many Caribbean islands. In Florida, big brown bats are not as common as in other portions of their range. In many northern states, the big brown bat and the little brown myotis (*Myotis lucifugus*)

Uncommon

Rare

are the most common species found roosting in buildings. The distribution of big brown bats in peninsular Florida has been previously shown to include only the northern two-thirds of the state, but over the past several years big brown bats have been found in Charlotte and Lee counties, and as far south as Naples in Collier County. Although there are no records of big brown bats in southeast Florida, more research could show them to be there as well. They have not been found in the Florida Keys.

Remarks. Because big brown bats adopt a wide variety of roost sites and roost in small colonies, at least in Florida, their populations are less vulnerable than some of Florida's species. However, their numbers in Florida are not large and therefore this species deserves some attention. Because they adopt buildings as roost sites, they are exposed to wanton and willful destruction by building owners and unnecessary deaths resulting from improperly conducted exclusions. Programs educating building owners and pest control operators on proper exclusion methods and the timing thereof are important for the continued well-being of this species.

Lasionycteris noctivagans

Silver-haired Bat

Description. The silver-haired bat is a medium-sized bat with dark brown to black fur. The fur has silvery white tips, giving it a frosted appearance. The tail membrane has a light covering of fur over the anterior half of the dorsal surface. The wing membranes and ears are black. The ears are short, broad, and rounded. The tragus is short and straight, with a rounded tip. The calcar is not keeled (Plate 3).

Roosting behavior. The silver-haired bat is primarily a solitary species but occasionally is found in small groups. Roost sites include hollow trees, spaces behind loose bark, tree cavities, rock crevices, and buildings. Unlike most species, which prefer the warm areas of buildings, silver-haired bats are more likely to be found in open structures such as sheds, open garages, and outbuildings. They are occasionally found roosting on the sides of buildings and other manmade structures.

	Measurements	Categories
Wingspan:	270–320 mm (12 inches)	Family: Vespertilionidae
Body length:	57–70 mm (2½ inches)	Florida occurrence: Accidental
Total length:	92–115 mm (4 inches)	Florida status: Rare
Forearm length:	36–45 mm	Roosting behavior: Solitary/Colonial
Weight:	8–16 g	Regional classification: Temperate

Foraging behavior. Silver-haired bats emerge from their roosts later than most species and exhibit a slower flight pattern. They feed on a diversity of small insects including moths, flies, beetles, termites, caddisflies, and true bugs. Silver-haired bats typically forage over and adjacent to water. They often fly close to the ground and around treetops.

One specimen found near Escambia River, September 1985

One specimen found on Bahia Honda Key, 1996

Reproduction. Silver-haired bats, like many other temperate species, are believed to mate in the fall. Females give birth from June through early July, after a gestation period of 50–60 days. They have been found in small nursery colonies in the cavities of trees. Females normally give birth to twins. Silver-haired bats are highly migratory, and it appears that the sexes may live in separate geographical regions during the summer months. They are not known to mate or give birth in Florida. Most births occur in Canada and northern parts of the United States.

Range. The silver-haired bat is found from Alaska and southern Canada south through most of the continental United States, and into northeastern Mexico. The southeastern portion of its range ends in southern Georgia and Alabama and does not normally include Florida.

Remarks. There have been only two documented findings of this species in Florida. One was a young adult female found in Santa Rosa County in the western panhandle in September 1985. The other was found in Bahia Honda State Park, a popular camping destination in the Lower Florida Keys. Silver-haired bats have been reported roosting in unusual places, such as the rolled awnings of RVs. They are a forest-dwelling species, and this individual could have been transported from a northern campground into Florida.

Lasiurus borealis

Eastern Red Bat

Description. The eastern red bat is a medium-sized bat with colorful fur. Males are more brightly colored than females. This is unusual, because color differences between males and females are rare among bat species. The fur of male red bats is brick red to reddish orange, or in some cases, yellowish red. Female

	Measurements	Categories
Wingspan:	280–330 mm (12 inches)	Family: Vespertilionidae
Body length:	51–61 mm (2¼ inches)	Florida occurrence: Resident
Total length:	90–123 mm (4¼ inches)	Florida status: Common in range
Forearm length:	35–45 mm	Roosting behavior: Solitary
Weight:	9–15 g	Regional classification: Temperate

red bats have a duller and lighter coloration. In both sexes, the tips of the hairs may be white, giving them a frosted appearance. Fur around the face is often lighter and yellowish. A patch of lighter-colored fur, often white, is found on the shoulders and wrists. The ears are short and rounded with a short, triangular tragus. The tip of the tragus curves forward and is rounded. The feet are small, measuring about 8 mm, and furred. The tail membrane is relatively long, measuring about 45 mm, with a heavily furred dorsal surface. The eastern red bat and the closely related Seminole bat appear identical in many ways, but can be distinguished by the color of their fur. Although in both species the fur may be tipped with white, the Seminole bat's fur is darker and more mahogany in color (Plate 4).

Roosting behavior. Like other bats in the genus *Lasiurus*, the eastern red bat is a solitary, tree-roosting species. It often hangs by one foot from the foliage of trees or bushes, or from a small branch or twig, giving it the appearance of a dead leaf. It tends to select a location within tree foliage that is concealed from the sides and above but unobstructed below, enabling it to drop freely and take flight. Preferred roost sites are usually at the edge of a clearing, lake, or stream. The eastern red bat is able to withstand cold temperatures by wrapping its long, thickly furred tail membrane around its underside and wings.

Foraging behavior. Eastern red bats feed on moths, beetles, mosquitoes, leafhoppers and planthoppers, flies, and other insects. They typically forage back and forth along tree lines, often above the tree tops, over streams, and around streetlights. Although they are considered aerial feeders, catching insects in flight, there have been observations of red bats gleaning insects by landing briefly on tree branches and light poles. There is also evidence that they may glean insects from the ground.

Reproduction. The time of mating in Florida is not known, but in northern states and Canada, eastern red bats mate during August and September. In Florida, they most likely mate during the fall with females storing the sperm until spring, when ovulation and fertilization take place. Females may give birth to one to four young. In Florida, the number is usually three or four. Birthing is typically in late May through mid-June. Young begin flying at 3–4 weeks and are fully weaned at 5–6 weeks.

Range. The eastern red bat is found in southern Canada, throughout the eastern United States, and in north-eastern Mexico. In Florida, eastern red bats are found mainly in the northern portion of the state, with their abundance decreasing toward the east coast and southward into the peninsula. Although eastern red bats are found year-round in north Florida, populations are thought to increase during winter months as bats migrate south from other states.

■ Common
▨ Uncommon

Remarks. Because eastern red bats are a tree-dwelling species, it is necessary to preserve hardwood forests in north Florida if we are to maintain populations of this species. Eastern red bats do not roost in manmade structures; therefore, bat houses will not compensate for loss of habitat.

Lasiurus cinereus

Hoary Bat

Description. The hoary bat is Florida's second-largest species. Its large size and distinctive fur make it easy to identify. The hoary bat's long, thick fur is a mix of colors, ranging from blackish brown to mahogany and cream. Most of the hairs are tipped with white, giving the bat a frosted appearance. The common name for this species comes from the term "hoarfrost," which is a coating of white frozen dew. Areas of the shoulders and wrists are highlighted with yellowish or white fur. Yellowish cream-colored fur also appears around the throat and face. Patches of yellowish or white fur appear on the underside of the shoulders and on the wrists at the base of the thumbs. The dorsal surface of the tail membrane is heavily furred, as are the feet. The ears are short and rounded and have a

	Measurements	Categories
Wingspan:	340–415 mm (15 inches)	Family: Vespertilionidae
Body length:	72–78 mm (3 inches)	Florida occurrence: Resident
Total length:	102–152 mm (5 inches)	Florida status: Rare
Forearm length:	46–58 mm	Roosting behavior: Solitary
Weight:	20–35 g	Regional classification: Temperate

distinctive black edge. The remarkable fur of the hoary bat makes it one of the world's most beautiful mammals (Plate 5).

Roosting behavior. Like other bats of the genus *Lasiurus*, the hoary bat is a solitary, tree-dwelling species. It typically roosts in tree foliage, but has also been found in tree cavities, in Spanish moss, behind loose bark, and on tree trunks, where it is amazingly well-camouflaged. In foliage, these bats tend to select a site concealed from the sides and above, but unobstructed below, enabling them to drop freely and take flight. It is found mostly in forested areas, where it often chooses roost sites in trees on the edges of clearings.

Like other species in the genus *Lasiurus*, the hoary bat can wrap its thickly furred tail membrane around its wings and underside while roosting. The hoary bat's thick fur is more insulative than other species, allowing it to withstand much colder temperatures. Hoary bats have been found foraging in temperatures as low as 32°F, and hibernating openly in tree roosts in temperatures well below freezing.

Foraging behavior. Hoary bats emerge later in the evening than most bats, although they have occasionally been seen flying in the late afternoon on warm winter days. They typically fly a straight, steady course after emerging, as they commute to their feeding area or a water source. Because of their size, hoary bats are capable of feeding on large insects. They appear to prefer moths, but also feed on beetles, flies, grasshoppers, mosquitoes, dragonflies, wasps, flying termites, and other insects.

Reproduction. In summer, female hoary bats are found in North America from southern Canada through the north central and eastern United States. Males are rarely found in these areas during summer, suggesting an interesting segregation of the sexes during the birthing season. Females with young have been found as far south as Georgia, but they have not been reported in Florida. Hoary bats can give birth to one to four young, but the usual number is two. Birthing takes place from mid-May through early July, depending on the latitude. The time of mating is unclear, and may occur before or during fall migration, or at wintering locations.

Rare

Range. The hoary bat is the most widespread bat in the Americas. It has been found as far north as northern Canada and as far south as Chile and Argentina. Hoary bats are found in all 50 states, including Hawaii, where it is their only endemic terrestrial mammal. Other locations where hoary bats have been found include Iceland, Bermuda, the Dominican Republic, the Galapagos, and the Orkney Islands.

In Florida, hoary bats have been found as far south as north central Florida. They have been found only during the months of October through April, and even then, findings are rare. Hoary bats are known to be highly migratory, but there is still much to learn about their migration patterns. Northern populations make long seasonal migrations to spend winter months in warmer climates.

Remarks. Because hoary bats are seldom encountered by people, there is little information about their presence or abundance in Florida. In the past, researchers have speculated that hoary bats migrated through Florida in the spring and fall. However, no specimens have been found in south Florida, suggesting that they do not pass through the state. Our current thinking is that hoary bats expand their range into Florida from the north during the cooler months of the year. However, because there are records of hoary bats in Georgia during summer, including females with young, it is possible that more research in north Florida may find them here during warmer months as well. Hoary bats have been categorized as resident in Florida, although they may be only seasonally resident. More work is justified to fully understand the migratory behaviors of hoary bats and their dependence on Florida habitat during winter months.

Lasiurus intermedius

Northern Yellow Bat

Description. The northern yellow bat is one of Florida's larger species. Its fur varies from yellowish brown to grayish brown. The tips of the fur are often slightly darker. Juveniles are less yellow in color, and appear more uniformly gray or light brown. Like other Florida species in the genus *Lasiurus* (red, Seminole, and hoary bats), the yellow bat has a furred tail membrane, yet it differs in that only the anterior half of the tail membrane is furred. There are no lighter patches of fur or white markings on the yellow bat like those found on Florida's other lasiurine species. Also, the ears are longer and more pointed, but the tra-

	Measurements	Categories
Wingspan:	350–410 mm (15 inches)	Family: Vespertilionidae
Body length:	70–72 mm (2¾ inches)	Florida occurrence: Resident
Total length:	121–132 mm (5 inches)	Florida status: Common
Forearm length:	45–56 mm	Roosting behavior: Solitary
Weight:	14–31 g	Regional classification: Temperate

gus is similarly short, with a rounded tip curving forward. Northern yellow bats have a slightly keeled calcar (Plate 6).

Roosting behavior. The northern yellow bat is a solitary tree-dwelling species. Sabal palm skirts and oaks with Spanish moss provide the roost sites for most of Florida's northern yellow bats, but other palms with thick skirts such as Washingtonia, and other trees with Spanish moss, are used by yellow bats as well. Although solitary, several individuals may roost in different areas of the same tree. Forested areas, especially oak and palm hammocks, are the natural habitat of yellow bats. They are also common in urban areas where the moss and palm skirts have been left undisturbed.

Foraging behavior. Northern yellow bats are known to feed on leafhoppers, flies, beetles, damselflies, and flying ants. They emerge about 15–20 minutes after sunset, and tend to fly a straight, steady course about 15–20 feet above ground, veering off to capture insects. They forage in a variety of habitats, but are commonly seen flying over open grassy clearings and along the edges of forested areas. In urban areas, they frequently forage around the lights of ball parks, along roads, and over golf courses.

Reproduction. Northern yellow bats mate in the fall, and possibly also during winter and early spring. Female yellow bats give birth from late May through June and, like other species within the genus *Lasiurus*, may have up to four pups. In Florida, they are most often found with three or four pups. During the day, the pups cling to the mother. She will then leave them behind in the evening as she forages for insects, occasionally returning to feed them during the night. She seldom attempts to fly with the young, unless disturbed or threatened. Because of the heavy load posed by her pups, female yellow bats often fall from their roost and are found on the ground after a windstorm or other disturbance with their pups still clinging to them.

Range. Northern yellow bats are found throughout the southeastern United States, and Cuba. Westward, their range extends into eastern Texas and south to Nicaragua. In the southeastern United States, the range of this species seems to coincide with that of sabal palms and Spanish moss. There have been a few isolated findings of this species in coastal Virginia and New Jersey. In Florida, they are found throughout the state except in the Florida Keys.

Common

Remarks. Although northern yellow bats are considered common throughout their range, they are heavily dependent on the preservation of rural and forested areas. Yellow bats are particularly vulnerable because of their limited roost preferences: dead palm fronds and Spanish moss. Consequently, they are becoming rare in urban areas where palm trees are overtrimmed and Spanish moss is removed or sprayed. To provide habitat for yellow bats, older oaks and tall sabal palms should be preserved. In areas where older tree growth exists, the palm skirts should be left in their natural untrimmed state and the Spanish moss allowed to accumulate. Trimming, if any, should be done with care. Yellow bats are often injured or killed by tree trimmers unaware of their presence. During the day, the bats are in torpor and cannot readily fly to escape danger. They may also be hesitant to leave the protection of their tree roost during daylight. Since these bats do not move into manmade structures, building bat houses will not compensate for loss of habitat.

Lasiurus seminolus

Seminole Bat

Description. The Seminole bat is a medium-sized bat with richly colored mahogany fur. In some individuals the tips of the fur are white, giving a slightly frosted appearance. Fur around the face is often lighter and more yellowish. Seminole bats have a patch of white or light-colored fur on the shoulders and wrists. The tail membrane is relatively long, with a thickly furred dorsal surface. The feet are small, measuring about 8 mm, and furred. The ears are short and rounded, with a tragus that tapers to a rounded tip and angles slightly forward. Seminole bats are closely related to red bats, *Lasiurus borealis*, and can appear identical except for color. The fur of Seminole bats is a darker brownish red color, while the fur of red bats is a brighter brick red to reddish yellow in males, and a lighter, more muted color in females (Plate 7).

Roosting behavior. The Seminole bat is a solitary, tree-roosting species. It is commonly found roosting in pine trees and in the clumps of Spanish moss on large oaks. The clumps of moss most often chosen are on the west or southwest edge of a clearing, where they receive the warmth of the late afternoon sun. The

	Measurements	Categories
Wingspan:	280–330 mm (12 inches)	Family: Vespertilionidae
Body length:	46–68 mm (2¼ inches)	Florida occurrence: Resident
Total length:	89–115 mm (4 inches)	Florida status: Common
Forearm length:	35–45 mm	Roosting behavior: Solitary
Weight:	9–14 g	Regional classification: Temperate

use of Spanish moss as a roost site is well-known, as Seminole bats are frequently found when people are removing moss from trees, or after a storm when moss has been blown down. Seminole bats are often associated with wooded areas, including pinelands, palm-oak hammocks, wetland forests, and river swamps. Their roost sites are rarely discovered in the trees of these habitats, because their mahogany color with slight silver frosting provides excellent camouflage.

Common
Uncommon

Foraging behavior. Seminole bats feed on moths, beetles, true bugs, flies, and other insects. They have also been reported feeding on flightless crickets. This suggests they may drop to the ground to catch insects, although this behavior appears to be rare. An observation was made of a Seminole bat circling a sabal palm and landing repeatedly for several seconds at a time while picking off insects that were feeding on the flower spikes. This feeding method, called gleaning, is likely rare for Seminole bats. Typically, they forage for insects in flight and can be seen flying back and forth along tree lines, often at treetop level. They may also be observed foraging for insects around street lights.

Reproduction. Seminole bats are known to mate in the fall, but reproductively active males have also been caught in February and April. Since Seminole bats are active year-round in Florida, it is likely that mating occurs in fall, winter, and spring. Like other bats in the genus *Lasiurus*, females may give birth to one to four young, but in Florida, the number is usually three or four. Most females give birth from mid-May through mid-June. The young begin to take their first flight at three to four weeks of age.

Range. Seminole bats are common in Florida and the southeastern United States. Their range extends west through parts of coastal Texas. There have been a few records of Seminole bats being found as far north as New York and Pennsylvania, but the northern extent of their range is normally North Carolina. Their range closely coincides with the distribution of Spanish moss and long leaf pine. In Florida, this species is found throughout the state except in the Florida Keys, but is not as abundant in the southern portions of the state.

Remarks. Because Seminole bats are heavily dependent on Spanish moss as roosting habitat, the protection of this epiphyte is important for their well-being. To provide Seminole bat habitat, older oaks should be preserved and Spanish moss allowed to accumulate. Since these bats do not move into manmade structures, building bat houses will not compensate for loss of habitat.

Myotis austroriparius

Southeastern Myotis

Description. The southeastern myotis is a small bat with dull, woolly-textured fur. The fur is bicolored, with the lower portion darker than the tips. Dorsally, the fur varies in color and can range from brown to gray and, occasionally, brownish orange. Ventrally, the fur is lighter, varying from tan to whitish. Long hairs extend between the toes and well beyond the claws. The calcar is not keeled (Plate 8).

Roosting behavior. The southeastern myotis is primarily a cave-dwelling bat, though often found in smaller colonies in hollow trees, buildings, bridges, culverts, bat houses, and similar structures. They often occupy caves along with eastern pipistrelles and, in north Florida, colonies of gray myotis. In manmade structures, southeastern myotis have been found roosting with evening bats and Brazilian free-tailed bats. The stable cave environment is critical for this species as a roost site during the maternity season. In the winter, caves provide important roosting habitat for some colonies, while others disperse to a variety of structures. Southeastern myotis do not appear to spend extended periods of time in hibernation, and their activity is thought to vary with insect activity and temperature.

Foraging behavior. Mosquitoes make up a large portion of the diet of southeastern myotis, especially during certain times of the year. Other insect prey includes moths, beetles, and crane flies. Southeastern myotis emerge at dusk and usually fly to ponds or streams, where they forage close to the surface of the water. They are thought to forage on all but the coldest nights of the year. Even in northern parts of the state they have been observed emerging from caves on winter nights.

Reproduction. Southeastern myotis are unique among myotis species in that females normally produce twins, whereas other myotis species usually give birth to only one young. Populations of southeastern myotis in the panhandle

	Measurements	Categories
Wingspan:	238–270 mm (10 inches)	Family: Vespertilionidae
Body length:	48–53 mm (2 inches)	Florida occurrence: Resident
Total length:	82–87 mm (3½ inches)	Florida status: Common in range
Forearm length:	36–41 mm	Roosting behavior: Colonial
Weight:	5–8 g	Regional classification: Temperate

follow the typical reproductive pattern of temperate species: mating in the fall, delaying fertilization, then giving birth in the spring. Mating has been observed, however, during the spring in panhandle populations. Peninsular populations mate in the spring from mid-February to mid-April. Females in both populations form maternity colonies in mid-March. The pups are born during the first three weeks of May, with the peak of birthing occurring in the second week. At birth, southeastern myotis pups are less developed than the pups of most species. The young begin to fly at five or six weeks of age. Males are rarely found in the same roost with females during the maternity season.

All significant maternity colonies of southeastern myotis are found within caves, and relatively few caves offer a microclimate suitable for successful reproduction. Maternity roosts must have warm, stable temperatures and high humidity, and be in close proximity to good foraging areas. Preferred caves have temperatures of 68–73°F (20–23°C) and domed areas where the colony can congregate, enabling their combined body heat to raise the temperature of the surrounding air to around 82°F (27°C). In the past, maternity colonies in Florida were normally found in caves with water under the roosting area, but today they are found using areas with no water beneath the roost site. This may be the result of changes in the water levels of Florida caves or loss of preferred caves due to disturbance.

Range. Southeastern myotis are more abundant in Florida than in other parts of their range. The range of this species extends northward to coastal North Carolina and westward through the Gulf States into the extreme eastern edge of Texas and southeastern Oklahoma. They have also been found in lesser numbers in the Mississippi Valley as far north as southern Illinois and Indiana. Their range in Florida is closely associated with the distribution of caves. They have

been found to a lesser extent further south, using other roost sites. In 1929, several southeastern myotis were found wintering in mangrove trees on Tampa Bay. Based on behavioral differences, it was once thought that populations of southeastern myotis in the panhandle were distinct from those in peninsular Florida. More likely they are not, but the differences in behavior may be a response to the transition in climate.

Common
Uncommon

Remarks. Historically, southeastern myotis have been known to use 19 caves in Florida as maternity roosts. A study by the Florida Game and Fresh Water Fish Commission during 1991 and 1992 found only nine caves occupied by maternity colonies. Of the other ten caves that were previously used, three had been deliberately sealed up by the landowners; three had had the surrounding forest cleared, which significantly altered the habitat; and three of the remaining four caves showed signs of vandalism. Even caves that were occupied at the beginning of the maternity season were found to be later vandalized, causing the bats to abandon the cave before successfully rearing their young. Fires had been set under two maternity colonies, and spent ammunition, along with the dead carcasses of adults and young, were found at a third cave.

Myotis grisescens

Gray Myotis

Description. The gray myotis is a medium-sized bat compared to other Florida species, yet it is one of the largest of the myotis species in North America. Its uniformly colored fur distinguishes it from other species in the genus *Myotis*. The individual hairs are gray, and do not vary in color from the base to the tip. Another distinguishing feature is that the wing membrane attaches at the ankle rather than at the base of the toe, as with other species of myotis. The calcar is not keeled (Plate 9).

Roosting behavior. The gray myotis is a cave-dwelling species and dependent on suitable cave environments for survival. Different types of caves are used during different seasons of the year. For winter hibernation, they choose cold caves where the air temperature is 43–52°F (6–11°C). Caves with these temperatures are rare; consequently, the entire North American population of gray myotis is believed to hibernate in as few as nine caves. In spring, gray myotis migrate to warm, humid caves with temperatures of 55–79°F (13–26°C). In Florida, females form maternity colonies in only two known caves. In the fall, most gray myotis in Florida migrate north, where they hibernate in caves in northern Alabama and Tennessee. A small and declining number of gray myotis remain during the winter in one or two Florida caves.

	Measurements	Categories
Wingspan:	270–320 mm (11 inches)	Family: Vespertilionidae
Body length:	41–57 mm (2 inches)	Florida occurrence: Resident
Total length:	80–96 mm (3½ inches)	Florida status: Endangered
Forearm length:	40–46 mm	Roosting behavior: Colonial
Weight:	8–10 g	Regional classification: Temperate

Foraging behavior. Gray myotis eat a variety of small insects including moths, beetles, flies, mosquitoes, and midges. They typically forage over streams, rivers, ponds, and lakes that are bordered by forests. They often use corridors within forested areas when traveling between their roost and foraging sites.

Rare

Reproduction. Mating takes place in the fall before migration to winter hibernacula. After mating, the females enter hibernation and store the sperm through the winter. They become pregnant after emerging from hibernation in the spring. They migrate from colder caves to warm, humid caves, where they form maternity colonies. These caves are usually large and contain deep water or streams. They typically choose a room within the cave that has a domed ceiling or is structured in a way that the air is trapped, allowing their combined body heat to raise the temperatures to levels suitable for gestation and rearing young. Female gray myotis usually give birth to a single pup in late May or June. The pups begin to fly at about three weeks of age. Both of the known gray myotis maternity colonies in Florida roost and rear their young along with large maternity colonies of southeastern myotis.

Range. In Florida, sizeable gray myotis colonies have been found only in the caves of Jackson County, although smaller colonies may be present in the caves of adjacent counties. North Florida caves mark the southernmost extreme end of the gray myotis range. Populations of gray myotis are also found in the cave regions of Missouri, Kentucky, Tennessee, Alabama, and Arkansas, and occasionally in adjacent states.

Remarks. The gray myotis is listed as endangered by both the Florida Fish and Wildlife Conservation Commission and the U.S. Fish and Wildlife Service. Because of the species' narrow criteria for the selection of cave roosts, there are only a few caves in Florida that qualify as gray myotis roost sites. Of these, only two caves are used as maternity sites, and the level of reproduction is uncertain. Continued vigilance will be needed in the management of these sites and the monitoring of the colonies. Protection of caves and foraging habitat in the Jackson County area is critical to the survival of this species in Florida.

Myotis septentrionalis
Northern Long-eared Myotis

Description. The northern long-eared myotis is a small bat, although it is medium sized compared to other myotis species. Its nonglossy fur is medium to dark brown dorsally, with lighter fur ventrally. The wing membranes and ears are dark brown. It has long ears, usually measuring more than 16 mm, which, when laid forward, extend just beyond the tip of the nose. The tragus is long, measuring about one-half the length of the ear, and sharply pointed. The calcar is not keeled (Plate 10).

Roosting behavior. The northern long-eared myotis hibernates in caves and mines. Although often found in the same roost site with other species, they seem to prefer the colder, more humid roost areas. They are often found hanging singly, wedged into tight crevices and holes; however, small groups of hibernating individuals have been found, usually numbering fewer than 100 individuals. Summer roosts and nursery colonies have been found under tree bark, behind shutters, and in buildings. Maternity colonies are small, usually ranging from several to 30 individuals.

Foraging behavior. Northern long-eared myotis emerge shortly after dusk. They usually forage under the forest canopy, just above shrub level, and over ponds and clearings at a height of about 3–10 feet. Northern long-eared myotis feed on a variety of small insects including moths, flies, leafhoppers, and beetles. In addition to catching insects in flight, they have been known to glean insects off twigs and foliage.

Reproduction. The northern long-eared myotis does not reproduce in Florida. Within its normal range, mating is believed to occur mainly in the fall, as is typical of temperate bat species. Females give birth to a single pup, from early May through early June. The young begin to fly in about five to six weeks.

Range. In Florida, this species is known from only one specimen, a female found hibernating in Old Indian Cave, Jackson County, in October 1954. After this finding, other nearby caves were searched, but no other specimens were found. The normal range for the northern long-eared myotis is from southeast-

	Measurements	Categories
Wingspan:	230–270 mm (10 inches)	Family: Vespertilionidae
Body length:	41–59 mm (2 inches)	Florida occurrence: Accidental
Total length:	74–96 mm (3 inches)	Florida status: Rare
Forearm length:	32–39 mm	Roosting behavior: Colonial
Weight:	5–10 g	Regional classification: Temperate

ern Canada through the central and eastern portions of the United States, as far south as Alabama and Georgia.

One specimen found in Old Indian Cave, October 1954

Remarks. It is unknown whether the single individual found in Old Indian Cave in 1954 was a remnant of a past population, or had wandered outside of the species' normal range. Old Indian Cave and other caves in that area have been surveyed for bats over the years, but this species has never been found since.

Myotis sodalis

Indiana Myotis

Description. The Indiana myotis is a small bat, yet medium in size compared to other myotis species. Its fur is fine and fluffy and can range in color from nearly black to light brown, but usually appears as a dull chestnut gray. Ventrally, the fur is dark gray at the base, and grayish white at the tips, with a cinnamon brown tinge giving the fur a pinkish appearance. The fur is dull rather than glossy, and may appear tricolored. The Indiana myotis has short, inconspicuous toe hairs that do not extend past the toes. The calcar has a small keel. The tragus is slightly less than half the length of the ear and has a blunt tip (Plate 11).

Roosting behavior. Indiana myotis spend the winter hibernating in caves and mines with cool, stable temperatures. They hang side-by-side, forming dense clusters of up to several thousand individuals when hibernating. In spring, females move to roosts in riparian areas, where they form small maternity colonies and roost in hollow trees, behind loose bark, and in similar cavities. Although some males remain at their hibernation cave sites during the summer,

	Measurements	Categories
Wingspan:	240–280 mm (10 inches)	Family: Vespertilionidae
Body length:	41–49 mm (1¾ inches)	Florida occurrence: Accidental
Total length:	73–100 mm (3½ inches)	Florida status: Endangered
Forearm length:	35–41 mm	Roosting behavior: Colonial
Weight:	6–10 g	Regional classification: Temperate

most disperse over a larger geographic area. Little is known about their summer roosting habitat.

Two specimens found in Old Indian Cave, October 1955

Foraging behavior. Indiana myotis feed mostly on soft-bodied insects such as moths, flies, and caddisflies, but at certain times of the year they also feed on beetles and other hard-bodied insects. They typically forage over streams and around the bordering trees, preferring streams with mature trees on both sides.

Reproduction. The Indiana myotis does not reproduce in Florida. Within their normal range, they mate primarily during a brief period in the fall before entering hibernation. They have occasionally been observed mating in the winter and also in late April upon leaving hibernation. Females typically give birth to a single pup in late June or early July.

Range. Indiana myotis are found in the cave regions of the eastern United States and in several Midwestern states. In winter, their populations are highly localized, with the known majority hibernating in only nine locations. In summer, they disperse throughout their range to riparian areas with nearby caves. In Florida, only two specimens have been found, both in Old Indian Cave, in October 1955. It is not known whether the two individuals were remnants of a larger or disjunct population that formerly occupied Old Indian Cave or whether they had simply strayed outside their normal range. Some range maps have shown an extension of the range southward into Florida based on these specimens. Although this may have been true at one time, these specimens, found 50 years ago, are far south of what is considered the present range of the Indiana myotis.

Remarks. The population of Indiana myotis continues to decline. It has all but disappeared from its summer range in the northeastern United States. Many caves previously serving as hibernacula now remain empty during the winter. It is estimated that the current population of Indiana myotis is fewer than 400,000. The Indiana myotis was one of the first bat species to be listed as endangered. The first recovery plan was approved in 1976 and revised in 1983, but despite efforts to protect it, the population continues to decrease. The decline is attributed to human disturbance at hibernation sites, loss of the mixed hardwood forests necessary for summer habitat, and pesticide poisoning. Unfortunately, these same hazards are impacting most North American bat species, regardless of whether or not they are classified as endangered.

Nycticeius humeralis

Evening Bat

Description. The evening bat is a small, darkly colored bat. Its fur is typically dark brown but may also have a bronze or reddish tint. Ventrally, the fur is a lighter, buff color. Juveniles, which are often encountered by people during the summer months, have very dark, nearly black fur. The evening bat has short, dark ears, with a short, rounded, and curved tragus. The muzzle is broad, dark, and unfurred, which distinguishes it from other small brown bats such as the myotis species, which have more pointed, furred muzzles. In overall appearance, this species resembles the big brown bat, but can be identified by its smaller size. A measurement of the adult forearm will easily distinguish it from the big brown bat (Plate 12).

Roosting behavior. Evening bats use a wide variety of roost sites, both natural and manmade. Their natural roosts consist primarily of dead trees and tree limbs. They roost in woodpecker cavities, behind loose bark, and in crevices caused by breaks and splits. They have occasionally been found roosting in Spanish moss. Evening bats utilize many types of manmade structures: buildings, where they may be in the eaves or soffits, in attics, behind signs or decorative fascia, or under barrel or flat tile roofs; bridges and stadiums, where they roost in cement crevices; utility poles, where they roost behind brackets that support transformers or street lights; and any similar structure where there is a small gap or crevice leading to an enclosed space. They are also commonly found in the folds of outdoor patio umbrellas. Evening bats readily move into bat houses and are the second most likely candidate for occupying a bat house in Florida.

Colony size usually ranges from just a few to around 70 individuals, although larger colonies have occasionally been found. Small colonies of evening bats often roost with larger colonies of Brazilian free-tailed bats, and occasionally with southeastern myotis.

	Measurements	Categories
Wingspan:	260–280 mm (10 inches)	Family: Vespertilionidae
Body length:	49–67 mm (2¼ inches)	Florida occurrence: Resident
Total length:	81–105 mm (3½ inches)	Florida status: Common
Forearm length:	33–39 mm	Roosting behavior: Colonial
Weight:	6–12 g	Regional classification: Temperate

Foraging behavior. Evening bats usually emerge from their roost about 15–20 minutes after sunset. They forage in a wide variety of environments, including open areas, over water, along tree lines, and around street lights. This species has strong jaws that enable them to feed on a wide variety of insects, including those with hard exoskeletons. They are known to eat flies, mosquitoes, beetles, moths, planthoppers, flying ants, and true bugs.

Common

Reproduction. Like other temperate species, evening bats are thought to mate in the fall. In Florida, mating behavior has also been observed in winter, as late as mid-February. Evening bats in Florida typically give birth during May, but birthing has been known to occur in late April. Female evening bats usually give birth to two pups, but may have from one to three.

Range. Evening bats are found throughout the eastern United States, but are most abundant in southeastern states. Their range extends west into east Texas and northeast Mexico. Although less common, they have been found as far north as Michigan and southern Ontario, and in some Midwestern states as far north as Nebraska. Evening bats are common throughout Florida, with the exception of the Florida Keys.

Remarks. Evening bats continue to be abundant in Florida. Because they adopt buildings as roost sites, they are exposed to wanton and willful destruction by building owners and to unnecessary deaths resulting from improperly conducted exclusions. Programs to educate building owners and pest control operators on proper exclusion methods and their timing are important for the well-being of this bat in urban areas. Preservation of wooded lands in Florida, including hardwoods and cypress swamps, is important for providing natural habitat for this species.

Pipistrellus subflavus

Eastern Pipistrelle

Description. The eastern pipistrelle is Florida's smallest bat species. Its fur varies in color from silvery gray to pale grayish yellow or light brown, although in more northern parts of its range, its fur may be darker or reddish brown. It is

	Measurements	Categories
Wingspan:	210–260 mm (9 inches)	Family: Vespertilionidae
Body length:	36–52 mm (2 inches)	Florida occurrence: Resident
Total length:	71–98 mm (3¼ inches)	Florida status: Uncommon
Forearm length:	31–36 mm	Roosting behavior: Colonial/Solitary
Weight:	6–8 g	Regional classification: Temperate

distinguished from other species by its tricolored fur; individual hairs are dark at the base, lighter in the middle, and dark at the tip. These three color bands can be seen when the fur is separated. In Florida, this characteristic is not always easy to recognize, as the tips of the fur are often very light in color and difficult to distinguish from the middle band. The anterior third of the dorsal surface of the tail membrane is sparsely furred. The skin on the forearms is light in color, often looking pinkish, contrasting with dark, blackish wing membranes. The ears are relatively long, measuring about 12–14 mm. If laid forward, the ears would extend just past the tip of the nose. The tragus is short and straight, tapering to a rounded point. The calcar is not keeled (Plate 13).

Roosting behavior. Eastern pipistrelles usually roost singly or in small groups. Habitats throughout their range include caves, mine shafts, tree foliage, tree cavities, rock crevices, Spanish moss, and occasionally, buildings. In Florida, they are often found in caves, but usually only during winter months. Rather than clustering together like colonial species, they are often found hanging singly or in pairs. In buildings (where they are only rarely found), they roost in open areas, exposed to more light than most other species would choose. Likewise, in caves they hang in the open, and are often found in more lit areas near the entrance. Although pipistrelles have occasionally been found in buildings, they have not yet been found roosting in bat houses.

Foraging behavior. Pipistrelles feed on small moths, flies, mosquitoes, leafhoppers, ants, and small beetles. Pipistrelles emerge early in the evening, just about sunset. They typically forage over water and along tree lines, flying erratically back and forth over a small area. With their slow flight and small size, they can easily be mistaken for a large moth.

Reproduction. In Florida, eastern pipistrelles mate in the fall, but it is possible that they also mate during winter and spring. In more northern states, they are believed to mate in the fall and spring. In Florida, the young are born during May and June, with the timing of births depending on latitude. Females usually give birth to two pups. The total fetal weight of the pups can equal a third or more of the mother's weight. The young grow quickly and begin to fly in about three weeks. The gestation period for eastern pipistrelles is about 45 days, which is slightly shorter than for other species in Florida.

Range. The eastern pipistrelle is widely distributed through the eastern United States and into Canada. Its range extends south around the Gulf of Mexico and into eastern Mexico, Guatemala, and Honduras. Although not considered abundant in Florida, eastern pipistrelles are found throughout the state, except in the Keys.

Uncommon

Remarks. Because pipistrelles roost in caves and forested areas, both habitat types need to be protected for their conservation. Programs to protect cave roosts for southeastern myotis will also benefit eastern pipistrelles, since they often roost within the same caves. Because they roost singly and in small groups, they have the advantage of using smaller caves as well, so the protection of even small caves known to serve as roosts for eastern pipistrelles would be advantageous. The preservation of hammocks and hardwood forests is important to provide the tree foliage, Spanish moss, and snags used by this species as roost sites. In rural areas, older oaks should be preserved and Spanish moss allowed to accumulate.

Family Molossidae

Bats of the family Molossidae are found primarily in the tropical and subtropical regions of the world, but they can also be found in the warmer portions of temperate regions as well. The family includes more than 16 genera and more than 90 species. Bats within the family Molossidae are also known as "free-tailed bats" because their tail extends well beyond a narrow tail membrane. Their faces are often doglike in appearance and, as a result, many are referred to as "mastiff" or "dog-faced" bats. The ears are often flat and protrude over the forehead like a bonnet. In fact, some species are referred to as "bonnetted bats." The eyes are small. The large upper lips are occasionally furrowed with vertical wrinkles. The fur is typically short and often velvety in texture and appearance. The outer toes often have long, bristlelike hairs. Many species have a throat gland, which, in some cases, exudes a strong musky odor. Although a few species are solitary, most are colonial and may form extremely large colonies. Molossid bats will go into torpor during colder periods, but there is no evidence of hibernation within this family. Some species migrate and others do not. All molossid species are insectivorous. They have long, narrow wings, and are high and fast flyers. Because of their high wing loadings, most have difficulty taking flight from the ground; when roosting, they tend to select a site that provides space for a long drop to gain speed for flight.

Eumops floridanus
Florida Bonneted Bat

Description. The Florida bonneted bat is the largest bat species in Florida. Its fur varies in color from dark gray to brownish gray or cinnamon brown on its dorsal side, with lighter, grayish fur underneath. The individual hairs are bicolored, being lighter at the base. Like other free-tailed bats in the family Molossidae, the tail of the Florida bonneted bat extends well beyond its short tail membrane. It has large, broad ears that slant forward over the eyes and are joined together at the midline of the head. This species is easily distinguished from Florida's other two molossid species by its large size (Plate 14).

Roosting behavior. Florida bonneted bats are found in both urban and forested areas. They are known to roost in rock crevices, tree cavities, and buildings. Like Brazilian free-tailed bats, one of their preferred roost sites is under barrel tile roofs. Recently, a colony was discovered roosting in a bat house in North Fort Myers. This is the first known occurrence of this species adopting a bat house as a roost site. They appear to roost only in small colonies of perhaps 8–12 individuals. Although information on social behavior comes from only two known colonies, findings suggest that they may roost in a "harem" structure consisting of one male with a group of females.

Foraging behavior. There has been little research on the diet of the Florida bonneted bat. Examination of the guano from one roost showed the remains of beetles, flies, and true bugs. The Florida bonneted bat emerges later in the evening than most Florida species. Observations at one roost site (the bat house) revealed that they emerge an average of 40 minutes after sunset. Bonneted bats are high, fast flyers and are often observed flying at 30 or more feet, foraging above treetops and over open areas such as golf courses.

	Measurements	Categories
Wingspan:	490–530 mm (20 inches)	Family: Molossidae
Body length:	84–108 mm (3¾ inches)	Florida occurrence: Resident
Total length:	130–165 mm (6 inches)	Florida status: Endangered
Forearm length:	61–66 mm	Roosting behavior: Colonial
Weight:	34–47 g	Regional classification: Tropical

Reproduction. Females give birth to a single pup, but they are believed to have two birthing seasons during the year. It has been speculated that one birthing period may occur in June and July, and a second in late summer. It is not known whether females produce an offspring in both birthing periods or whether most give birth only once during the year. Pregnant females have been found in June, July, August, and September. Since bonneted bats are so rarely encountered, there is still much to be learned about mating behaviors, the length of gestation, the timing of births, and weaning of the young.

Rare

Range. At one time, *Eumops glaucinus*, commonly referred to as Wagner's mastiff bat, was considered a single species throughout its extensive range. In 1971, the Florida population was recognized as a separate subspecies by Karl Koopman and given the scientific name of *Eumops glaucinus floridanus*. Bats in the Florida population are significantly larger in size, and the skull is noticeably different. Taxonomic research completed in 2004 by Robert Timm and Hugh Genoways has now concluded that the Florida population is, in fact, a distinct species and consequently has been reclassified as *Eumops floridanus* and referred to as the Florida bonneted bat.

Although appearing in the fossil record, this species was virtually unknown in Florida until the influx of development began in southeast Florida in the 1920s. The first specimen was found in the Miami area in 1936. When Jennings conducted his survey of Florida bats in the 1950s, he defined the range as being Coral Gables, Coconut Grove, and Miami. In 1979, a colony was found in an area of pine flatwoods in Punta Gorda in Charlotte County. This was the first record of the species on the west coast of Florida. No additional evidence was found of this species on the west coast until 2000, when its echolocation calls were recorded near Dismal Key in the 10,000 Islands and a skull was found in an owl pellet at Fakahatchee Strand. In February 2003, a colony was found roosting in a bat house in North Fort Myers. Based on these findings, the current range of the Florida bonneted bat is known to include both the east and west coasts of the southern portion of the Florida peninsula. To date, the species has not been found in the Florida Keys.

Plate 1. *Corynorhinus rafinesquii*, Rafinesque's big-eared bat (photo by J. Scott Altenbach).

Plate 2. *Eptesicus fuscus*, Big brown bat (photo by J. Scott Altenbach).

Plate 3. *Lasionycteris noctivagans*, Silver-haired bat (photo by J. Scott Altenbach).

Plate 4. *Lasiurus borealis*, Eastern red bat (photo by J. Scott Altenbach).

Plate 5. *Lasiurus cinereus*, Hoary bat (photo by J. Scott Altenbach).

Plate 6. *Lasiurus intermedius*, Northern yellow bat (photo by J. Scott Altenbach).

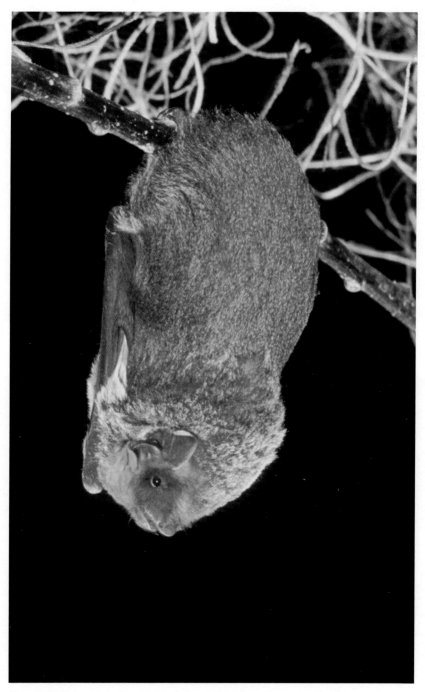

Plate 7. *Lasiurus seminolus*, Seminole bat (photo by J. Scott Altenbach).

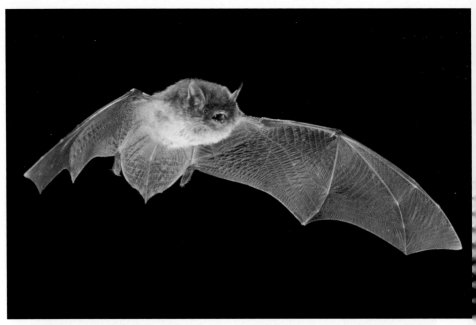

Plate 8. *Myotis austroriparius*, Southeastern myotis (photo by J. Scott Altenbach).

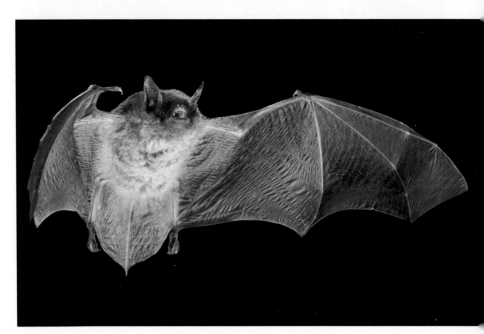

Plate 9. *Myotis grisescens*, Gray myotis (photo by J. Scott Altenbach).

Plate 10. *Myotis septentrionalis*, Northern long-eared myotis (photo by J. Scott Altenbach).

Plate 11. *Myotis sodalis*, Indiana myotis (photo by J. Scott Altenbach).

Plate 12. *Nycticeius humeralis*, Evening bat (photo by J. Scott Altenbach).

Plate 13. *Pipistrellus subflavus*, Eastern pipistrelle (photo by J. Scott Altenbach).

Plate 14. *Eumops floridanus*, Florida bonneted bat (photo by J. Scott Altenbach).

Plate 15. *Molossus molossus*, Velvety free-tailed bat (photo by J. Scott Altenbach).

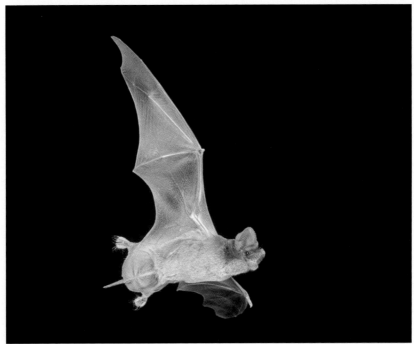

Plate 16. *Tadarida brasiliensis*, Brazilian free-tailed bat (photo by J. Scott Altenbach).

Plate 17. *Artibeus jamaicensis*, Jamaican fruit-eating bat (photo by J. Scott Altenbach).

Plate 18. *Erophylla sezekorni*, Buffy flower bat (photo by Barry Mansell).

Plate 19. *Phyllonycteris poeyi*, Cuban flower bat specimen found on Stock Island in 2002 (photo by George Marks).

Plate 20. *Phyllops falcatus*, Cuban fig-eating bat (photo by CourtneyPlatt.com).

Remarks. The species *Eumops glaucinus floridanus,* now *Eumops floridanus,* currently is listed as endangered by the Florida Fish and Wildlife Conservation Commission (FWC). In 1996, the U.S. Fish and Wildlife Service (USFWS) dropped *E. g. floridanus* as a candidate for federal protection. This, however, was while the bat was considered a subspecies of the greater population of *E. glaucinus*. Based on the reclassification of this bat as a unique species endemic to Florida, it is recommended that the agency provide federal protection for this species. Because of its limited range, rarity within that range, and declining population, the Florida bonneted bat is certainly a candidate for federal protection.

Molossus molossus

Velvety Free-tailed Bat

Description. The velvety free-tailed bat is a medium-sized bat found in the Florida Keys. Like other bats in the family Molossidae, the tail extends far beyond the tail membrane. Its short, velvety fur is darker dorsally, and varies in color from dark brown to dark gray. Its ears are joined at the midline of the head, a feature that distinguishes it from the similar-sized Brazilian free-tailed bat. Although not apparent in all individuals, velvety free-tailed bats have femoral hairs about 8–10 mm in length that extend upward from the hip area (Plate 15).

Roosting behavior. In Florida, the velvety free-tailed bat has been found only in buildings, where roost sites include attic spaces, walls, crevices, and eaves. In Cuba, they are primarily found in buildings, but are also found in tree hollows, rock crevices, and cracks in utility poles. They normally roost in large colonies. In Cuba, the major colonies range from four to five thousand bats, but smaller colonies of five to fifteen hundred are also fairly common. The largest colony found in Florida so far numbered just over thirteen hundred.

Foraging behavior. Velvety free-tailed bats emerge early in the evening, leaving the roost usually at sunset while the sky is still light. Although their diet has

	Measurements	Categories
Wingspan:	255–290 mm (11 inches)	Family: Molossidae
Body length:	59–65 mm (2½ inches)	Florida occurrence: Resident
Total length:	93–100 mm (3¾ inches)	Florida status: Uncommon
Forearm length:	32–38 mm	Roosting behavior: Colonial
Weight:	7–15 g	Regional classification: Tropical

not been studied in Florida, in Cuba they feed on planthoppers, leafhoppers, grasshoppers, moths, beetles, mayflies, and other small flying insects. Their high-aspect-ratio wings (long and narrow) enable them to be fast and high fliers. Velvety free-tailed bats chase and capture insects using swooping maneuvers much like swifts. They forage at the peak of insect activity after sunset, and again before dawn. Between feeding periods, they usually return to their day roost.

Uncommon

Reproduction. Velvety free-tailed bats are polyestrous. Although the timing of reproduction has not been studied in Florida, it is most likely the same as that of Cuban populations. In Cuba, most mating occurs in December and January. The first pups are born in June. A second reproductive cycle follows, so while lactating and raising one pup, females may also become pregnant again and give birth to a second pup later in the summer. Not as many females give birth during the second birthing period. Females usually give birth to a single pup.

Range. Velvety free-tailed bats are common in Cuba and throughout most of the Caribbean. They also have a wide distribution from northern Argentina through Central America and into Mexico. In Florida, velvety free-tailed bats are found only in the Florida Keys. The first colony was discovered in Marathon (Key Vaca) in 1994, with subsequent colonies found on Boca Chica, Stock Island, Sugarloaf Key, and Key West. By 2000, there were colonies on every major key in the Lower Keys. In 2004, a colony was found in the Upper Keys on Plantation Key.

Remarks. Because these bats are adopting buildings as roost sites in the Florida Keys, there will be many attempted exclusions. One of the problems associated with the exclusion of this species is that they have two birthing seasons; thus unflighted young may be found in the roost for a longer period of time than most other Florida species. This results in only a small window of time during which exclusions may be conducted. Performing exclusions during maternity seasons will trap the young inside, causing them to die of dehydration and starvation.

Until the appearance of this species, it had not been necessary to bat-proof buildings in the Keys, so there are likely many buildings receptive to bats in the area. Educational programs and materials are needed to provide Keys' residents with accurate information about bats, how to prevent their entry, and how to properly conduct exclusions. As buildings are bat-proofed, bat houses should be constructed as alternate roost sites. Bat houses for this species have proven successful on Grand Cayman Island and Puerto Rico. It seems that Clyde Perky's dream of using bats to help control insects in the Florida Keys has finally come true. It is now up to the residents of the Keys to provide the roost sites needed to retain these natural insect exterminators.

Tadarida brasiliensis
Brazilian Free-tailed Bat

Description. The Brazilian free-tailed bat is a medium-sized bat. Its fur is short and varies in color from dark brown to grayish brown. When at rest approximately half of the tail extends beyond the tail membrane, but in flight, the membrane can slide much further along the tail. The ears are broad and rounded and almost meet at the midline of the head, but they are not joined together, as they are in Florida's other two molossid species. The upper lips have vertical wrinkles or furrows. Long, stiff hairs protruding from the toes extend beyond the claws. The first and fifth toes have short bristles along their outer edges. The Brazilian free-tailed bat has a scent gland located at the base of the throat that secretes a strong, musky odor. A colony of Brazilian free-tailed bats can often be identified from a distance by this odor (Plate 16).

Roosting behavior. The rarity of Brazilian free-tailed bat fossils in Florida cave deposits suggests that, like today, they did not roost in Florida caves. It is thought they were most likely using the hollows of dead trees. Today it is extremely rare to find them in natural habitats and it seems they have abandoned their natural roosts in favor of manmade structures. In Florida, they are commonly found roosting in bridges, stadiums, attics, picnic shelters, eaves, soffits, and barrel tile roofs. They tend to choose very warm roost sites and are often found in barrel tile roofs year-round in Florida. Brazilian free-tailed bats form large colonies numbering in the thousands, depending on the availability of space within a roost site. Because of their abundance and preference for manmade structures, Brazilian free-tailed bats are the most likely candidates to

	Measurements	Categories
Wingspan:	290–325 mm (12 inches)	Family: Molossidae
Body length:	57–74 mm (2½ inches)	Florida occurrence: Resident
Total length:	90–109 mm (3¾ inches)	Florida status: Common
Forearm length:	36–46 mm	Roosting behavior: Colonial
Weight:	10–15 g	Regional classification: Tropical

move into bat houses just about anywhere in Florida. Other species of
bats, primarily evening bats, southeastern myotis, and big brown bats,
are often found roosting along with
Brazilian free-tailed bat colonies.

Common

Brazilian free-tailed bats in Texas,
Arizona, and New Mexico exhibit
much different roosting behaviors.
They roost in caves in Central Mexico during the winter and migrate
to caves in the southwestern United
States in spring; there they form
extremely large maternity colonies
numbering in the millions. Although Brazilian free-tailed bats in Florida may
move seasonally from one roost site to another, they do not migrate long distances.

Foraging behavior. Brazilian free-tailed bats usually emerge about 15–20 minutes after sunset. They are high, fast flyers and forage primarily over open areas.
They are known to eat a variety of insects, including moths, flies, and beetles.
Because they are fast flyers, they can travel long distances to reach foraging
areas, and large colonies may spread out over many miles. In some areas of the
country, they have proven to be a major controller of agricultural pests.

Reproduction. Mating is believed to occur in March, primarily during a three-
week period when the females are ovulating. Gestation lasts about 11–12 weeks.
With few exceptions, females give birth to a single pup in early June. Although
a colony of females may give birth to young over a 2–3-week period, the majority of births within a colony will occur in a five-day window. Free-tailed pups
begin flying at about 5–6 weeks of age, which is 2–3 weeks later than that of
many vespertilionid bats. Their higher wing loadings may demand stronger
wing muscles before their first flights can be safely launched.

Range. The Brazilian free-tailed bat is likely the most abundant bat in Florida,
and is found in all parts of the state except the Florida Keys. The greater range
of the Brazilian free-tailed bat extends from northern South America through
the Caribbean and Central America, Mexico, and the southern United States.
Brazilian free-tailed bats found in the United States have historically been classified as two subspecies: *Tadarida brasiliensis mexicanus*, commonly referred to
as the Mexican free-tailed bat, which occurs from eastern Texas westward, and
T. b. cynocephala, which occurs from eastern Texas through the southeastern

United States. Whether or not these should be listed as separate subspecies has often been a topic of debate, and genetic work is continuing to determine their relationship.

Remarks. Although Brazilian free-tailed bats are common in Florida and have adopted a diversity of manmade roosts, their roosting habits make them vulnerable. Rather than roosting in scattered small colonies, they congregate in large colonies. This often means that all of the bats in a given area may be roosting together in a single location. Although illegal, destruction of colonies is often done intentionally by extermination or inadvertently through improper exclusion methods. To conserve this species, wildlife professionals and pest control operators should be educated on proper exclusion methods and their timing with respect to the maternity season. It is important that buildings be designed and maintained to prevent them from becoming bat roosts. It is equally important, however, that structures where they create no problem, such as bridges and bat houses, be used to provide alternative roosting habitat.

Family Phyllostomidae

The family Phyllostomidae is unique to the tropical and subtropical regions of the New World (North America, South America, and the Caribbean). It includes more than 48 genera and more than 150 species. Most species have a prominent cartilaginous appendage on the tip of the nose, resembling a leaf. This forms the basis of their family name, which comes from the Greek word *phyllo*, meaning "leaf." Consequently, the family is often referred to as the "New World leaf-nosed bats." This family encompasses a diversity of bats, including one of the largest species of microchiropteran bats, the false vampire bat (*Vampyrum spectrum*), with a wingspan of more than three feet. Phyllostomid species feed on a wide variety of food sources, including fruit, nectar, pollen, and insects, and a few species feed on small mammals, lizards, frogs, and birds. This family also includes the three species of true vampire bats, the only bat species that feed on blood. Phyllostomid bats issue their echolocation calls through their nose rather than their mouth. They use the nose-leaf to aim or focus the sound. The echolocation calls of these bats are very faint and, consequently, they are often referred to as "whispering bats." Some species are colonial and others are solitary. Colonial species may roost in small groups or in very large colonies. A few species are migratory. None hibernate, and phyllostomid bats rarely, if ever, go into torpor.

Artibeus jamaicensis

Jamaican Fruit-eating Bat

Description. The Jamaican fruit-eating bat is a relatively large species with a prominent nose-leaf and large eyes. It has thick, soft fur that, on the dorsal side, varies from dull brown to grayish in color, and may exhibit a slight silvery sheen. The underside is somewhat paler. The Jamaican fruit-eating bat lacks an external tail and has a narrow uropatagium. Bats in the genus *Artibeus* often have pronounced white stripes running along the face above and below the eyes, but these stripes are usually muted or not obvious on Jamaican fruit-eating bats (Plate 17).

Roosting behavior. Jamaican fruit-eating bats roost in caves, rock overhangs, tree foliage, hollow trees, rock crevices, and manmade structures. They are a colonial species and usually roost in small groups of a dozen or so individuals. These groups may be clusters of males, females, or harems consisting of a single male and several females. No roost sites or evidence of colonization has been found in Florida.

Foraging behavior. Jamaican fruit-eating bats feed on fruit, pollen, nectar, flowers, leaves, and occasionally, insects. Their favorite fruits include figs, bananas, avocados, sapodilla, and mangoes. Because of this, they often have a pleasant fruity odor. They do not feed on citrus fruit. Jamaican fruit-eating bats squeeze the soft fruit in their mouths, swallow the juice, and spit out the pulp. Because of this, they prefer soft, ripe, juicy fruits. They usually carry the fruit in their mouths to a nearby tree to eat it. In a given foraging area, individual bats develop favorite roost sites for this purpose. When sunrise approaches, they frequently carry fruit back to their permanent roost site. As a result, the ground under their roosts becomes littered with piles of sticky fruit pulp, guano, and seeds.

Reproduction. Jamaican fruit-eating bats have more than one reproductive cycle per year. This species is found in many geographical areas with varying climates and seasons. Consequently, their reproductive cycles and mating strategies vary in different portions of their range to coincide with the timing and

	Measurements	Categories
Wingspan:	340–445 mm (15 inches)	Family: Phyllostomidae
Body length:	75–85 mm (3¼ inches)	Florida occurrence: Accidental
Total length:	75–85 mm (3¼ inches)	Florida status: Rare
Forearm length:	50–63 mm	Roosting behavior: Colonial
Weight:	27–45 g	Regional classification: Tropical

abundance of fruit. In Cuba, this species exhibits two reproductive cycles. There is a peak of birthing in April, and another in July and August. Females may give birth to one pup in each cycle, but fewer females become pregnant during the second cycle.

One specimen found in Key West, June 1995
One specimen found in Key West, March 1996

Range. Jamaican fruit-eating bats are widely distributed through the Caribbean, central and southern Mexico, Central America, and as far south as Bolivia, Paraguay, and Central Brazil. In Florida, only two specimens have been found, both in Key West. The closest populations to Florida are in Cuba, where it is considered a common species.

Remarks. Jamaican fruit-eating bats were first confirmed in Florida in 1995, when a specimen was found in Key West. A second specimen was also found in Key West in 1996. Both individuals were debilitated and died shortly after being collected. Prior to this, there had been sightings of bats described as resembling phyllostomid species. C. J. Maynard reported a bat he identified as an *Artibeus* species in 1870, but the identification was later disputed. A photograph taken of a bat in the East Martello Tower of Key West in 1983 was initially identified as a Jamaican fruit-eating bat, but this, also, was later disputed. There have been no additional specimens of *Artibeus* found in the Keys, but it would not be surprising if others are found in the future. It was once thought that a population of these bats could not survive in the Florida Keys because of the lack of year-round food sources. However, with the introduction of fruiting and flowering plants from Cuba and around the world, the possibility of this species surviving in the area is more likely.

Erophylla sezekorni

Buffy Flower Bat

Description. The buffy flower bat is a medium-sized species with a prominent nose-pad and a small nose-leaf. The nose-leaf is forked or notched at the tip. Its dorsal fur is distinctly bicolored: the lower portion is whitish, and the tips are a light brown. The overall appearance of the fur can be a pale yellowish brown or buffy color. Hairs on the face are shorter, uniformly colored, and appear nearly white. The fur on the underside is bicolored, and is much lighter in color than

	Measurements	Categories
Wingspan:	300–340 mm (12 inches)	Family: Phyllostomidae
Body length:	65–75 mm (2¾ inches)	Florida occurrence: Accidental
Total length:	77–92 mm (3¼ inches)	Florida status: Rare
Forearm length:	42–55 mm	Roosting behavior: Colonial
Weight:	13–21 g	Regional classification: Tropical

the dorsal fur. The tail is short and extends beyond the tail membrane. The narrow tail membrane attaches at the ankle. A small (1–2 mm) calcar is present. It can be difficult to differentiate between the buffy flower bat and the Cuban flower bat, another accidental phyllostomid species that has been found in the Florida Keys. The presence of the calcar, the attachment of the tail membrane at the ankle, and a tibia measurement that is less than half the length of the forearm distinguish this species from the Cuban flower bat (Plate 18).

Roosting behavior. The buffy flower bat is a colonial, cave-dwelling species. It forms colonies consisting of a few hundred to several thousand bats, roosting singly or in clusters. They are found both in the dark interior portions of caves and in areas where daylight enters. No roost sites have been found in Florida.

Foraging behavior. In the Bahamas, buffy flower bats have been observed leaving their roost just after sunset, yet in Cuba they have been reported leaving roosts an hour or more after sunset. They fly slowly and low as they forage around vegetation. Buffy flower bats feed on fruit, pollen, nectar, and insects. The long, extendable tongue with its bristlelike projections is especially adapted for feeding on pollen and nectar, yet a recent study in Puerto Rico and observations in the Bahamas indicate their diet consists more heavily of fruit.

Reproduction. Mating occurs from mid-November to mid-January. Although both males and females can be found roosting together in caves year-round, females may separate from males during the maternity season. Most births occur in June, with females giving birth to a single pup. The young reach adult size by late October, and all are weaned by the end of October.

Range. The buffy flower bat is resident throughout the Greater Antilles. In Florida, a dead specimen was found washed up on a

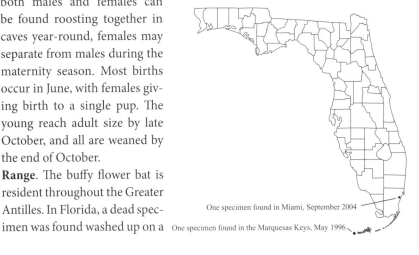

One specimen found in Miami, September 2004

One specimen found in the Marquesas Keys, May 1996

beach in the Marquesas (a group of islands east of the Dry Tortugas and west of Key West) in 1996, but was likely dead prior to arriving on Florida shores. In 2001, a bat was photographed on Elliot Key in Biscayne National Park. From the photograph, it was identified as the buffy flower bat. In 2004, a live specimen was found in Miami.

Remarks. The presence of a live specimen raises the question as to whether or not this species is residing in Florida. The individual was found shortly after four hurricanes had hit Florida, at least two of which could have created sufficient turbulence in the area to carry a wayward bat to Florida from the Bahamas or Cuba.

Phyllonycteris poeyi

Cuban Flower Bat

Description. The Cuban flower bat is a medium-sized species. It has a prominent nose-pad, but the nose-leaf, typical of phyllostomid bats, may be either small or absent. Its dorsal fur is distinctly bicolored: the lower portion is whitish, and the tips are grayish brown. The fur is silky and can produce silvery reflections. The overall appearance can be brownish with gray highlights. The underside is lighter in color. The tail is short and extends beyond the tail membrane. The tail membrane attaches to the tibia above the ankle and there is no calcar. The Cuban flower bat can be difficult to distinguish from the buffy flower bat, another accidental phyllostomid species that has been found in south Florida. The absence of a calcar, the attachment of the tail membrane above the ankle and a tibia measurement equal to half the length of the forearm or greater distinguish this species from the buffy flower bat (Plate 19).

Roosting behavior. The Cuban flower bat is a colonial, cave-dwelling species. Colonies may consist of many thousands of individuals. It is usually found in "hot caves," where temperatures can reach 104°F (40°C) and humidity ranges between 90 and 99 percent. No roost sites have been found in Florida.

Foraging behavior. Cuban flower bats leave their roosts late in the evening, usually an hour or more after sunset, to forage. They tend to forage during the darker periods of the night, when there is little or no moonlight. They fly slowly

	Measurements	Categories
Wingspan:	294–350 mm (12 inches)	Family: Phyllostomidae
Body length:	64–83 mm (3 inches)	Florida occurrence: Accidental
Total length:	71–95 mm (3¼ inches)	Florida status: Rare
Forearm length:	43–51 mm	Roosting behavior: Colonial
Weight:	15–29 g	Regional classification: Tropical

and low as they forage around vegetation. They feed mainly on pollen and nectar, but may also feed on other plant material, fruit, small flightless insects, and larvae. The long, extendable tongue with its bristlelike projections facilitates feeding on pollen and nectar.

One specimen found in Key West, 2001
One specimen found on Stock Island, November 2002

Reproduction. Mating most likely occurs in December. Although both males and females are found in the same caves year-round, females move to other areas of the cave during the maternity season. Females give birth to one pup per year, with most births occurring in June. The young reach adult size by late September, and all are weaned by the end of October.

Range. The Cuban flower bat is normally found only in Cuba, including the Isle of Pines. However, two specimens have been confirmed in Florida: one in Key West in 2001, and one on Stock Island in 2002. A small group of bats was found in the East Martello Tower of Key West in 1983. One was photographed and initially identified as a Jamaican fruit-eating bat, but a later examination indicates it was more likely a Cuban flower bat. A specimen photographed on Lignumvitae Key in 1984 was also identified as likely being the Cuban flower bat.

Remarks. Research is continuing to determine if there is a year-round population of this species in the Florida Keys. The introduction of fruiting and flowering plants in the Florida Keys may provide a year-round source of food, but the absence of caves or equivalent roost sites would likely limit the potential for colonization.

Phyllops falcatus

Cuban Fig-eating Bat

Description. The Cuban fig-eating bat is a medium-sized species with a prominent nose-leaf. Its dense fur is brownish gray and is darker dorsally. On the shoulder, near the point where the wing membrane joins the body, there is a tuft of white fur. The tragus is without pigment and appears yellowish, as does the skin inside the lower one-third of the ear. On most bats, the second and third fingers, which form the leading edge of the wing, are very close together. In this

	Measurements	Categories
Wingspan:	315–365 mm (13 inches)	Family: Phyllostomidae
Body length:	52–65 mm (2 inches)	Florida occurrence: Accidental
Total length:	52–65 mm (2 inches)	Florida status: Rare
Forearm length:	39–48 mm	Roosting behavior: Solitary
Weight:	16–23 g	Regional classification: Tropical

species, the second finger is curved forward, creating a much larger area between the two fingers. The wing membrane between these two fingers is translucent and has a paperlike appearance. These two digits remain separated, and the membrane taut, even when the bat is at rest. The Cuban fig-eating bat lacks an external tail, and has a narrow uropatagium. The tail membrane, feet, and toes are furred. The calcar is short, measuring 3–5 mm (Plate 20).

Roosting behavior. The Cuban fig-eating bat is a solitary, foliage-roosting species. In Cuba, they have been observed roosting in mahogany trees. They choose areas of trees that are thick with branches and dense foliage. Occasionally they are found in pairs or even in small groups of three to five individuals, but this behavior is believed to be related to the mating season.

Foraging behavior. Cuban fig-eating bats feed on fruit, but little is known about their foraging habits. In Cuba, they are known to feed on figs, rose apples, and fruits from trees in the genus *Cecropia*, but likely feed on many other small fruits as well. They are active throughout the night. In Cuba, individuals have been observed foraging as early as several minutes before sunset. They fly slowly, much like a butterfly, around vegetation. In Cuba, males and females have been observed flying in pairs.

Reproduction. Like many tropical species, Cuban fig-eating bats are believed to have more than one reproductive cycle per year. They give birth to a single pup, but may produce two young annually. Within their normal range, pregnant females have been found from December through June. As is typical of fruit bats, birthing and lactation likely coincide with the abundance of fruit.

Range. Cuban fig-eating bats are found in Cuba, Hispaniola, and on

One specimen found on Stock Island, February 2005

Grand Cayman Island. They are extremely rare on Grand Cayman, and until a small group was discovered in 2000, they were thought to be extinct on the island. Only one specimen has been found in Florida.

Remarks. The one specimen found in Florida was discovered and photographed in the Key West Tropical Forest and Botanical Gardens on Stock Island by a group of Duke University students in December of 2004. The bat had established a night roost in the foliage of an Arjuna almond tree (*Terminalia arjuna*). Staining in the area indicated it had been using the roost for some time. A search for the bat in February 2005 found it in the same location, in the same tree. Increased staining suggested the bat had been continuing to use the roost in the interim. It was captured, identified, photographed, and released. The bat was observed on several occasions over the following months roosting and foraging in the same general area. It would emerge from a cluster of mahogany trees shortly after sunset and was observed feeding on the fruit of a short-leaf fig (*Ficus citrifolia*).

6

Bat Conservation in Florida

For no bat species in Florida can it be said, there are no concerns about its future. Cave-dwelling bats are of concern because of the limited numbers of caves in Florida and their susceptibility to human disturbances. Foliage-dwelling bats are of concern because development in Florida has destroyed much of their natural habitat and continued development is expected. Bats that move into buildings are of concern because of illegal exterminations and improperly conducted exclusions. Very little is known about the current abundance of most species and, except for a few species, almost nothing is known about their population trends. A past lack of concern about bats, widespread misunderstanding, and the urgent needs of other wildlife have placed bat conservation in Florida in a "catch-up" mode.

Public Education

The major threat to bats over the last two centuries has been fear and misunderstanding. Bats are a part of Florida's natural wildlife and should be thought of no differently than songbirds and squirrels, but unfortunately, myth and legend have destined them to be associated with vampires and Halloween. Consequently, the average person's initial response to encountering a bat is fear and prejudice, rather than curiosity and respect. Because of this, most bat conservation organizations consider public education to be their number one priority. Through educational programs people can begin to understand the unique characteristics of bats, their actual size and appearance, the truth about rabies, the environmental benefits of bats, and how to properly deal with bats in buildings. Bats can also be used as a platform for teaching scholastic topics such as the physics of sound, the physics of flight, adaptive biology, ecology, and the importance of conservation.

Unfortunately, even when people take the time to search for accurate answers to bat-related questions, they stumble across incorrect, misleading, and in some cases, malicious information. Animal trappers and pest control operators often find it to their advantage to present fearful and horrific stories about the consequences of bats in buildings. People with little or no knowledge about bats

Figure 6.1. Exhibits and programs help educate the public about bats (photo by George Marks).

often pass on the traditional myths and misinformation prevalent in our society. This reinforces ignorance, since the more frequently the myths are heard, the more likely they are believed. The Internet, as with everything else, contains both good and bad information about bats. There are even instances when governmental agencies have conveyed inaccurate information because their employees have not been educated regarding bats. Governmental staff members are assumed by the public to be the experts on any topic within their area of jurisdiction. Consequently, it is imperative that they have accurate information regarding bats, particularly with respect to bats in buildings and bats and human health.

The good news is that public sentiment is changing. Organizations have been formed specifically for bat conservation. Documentaries about the unique characteristics and behaviors of bats have aired on national television. Teachers are including educational units on bats in their curricula. Recent children's storybooks are now portraying bats in a friendlier light. In time, the average person may view bats differently, but like any other prejudice, it is a slow process.

Preservation of Natural Habitat

The best strategy for protecting any plant or animal is the preservation of adequate natural habitat. Bats, however, are seldom thought of when lands are being considered for preservation or when management plans are being developed for lands that have been preserved. Fortunately, bats benefit from natural lands set aside for other purposes and survive with minimal attention in a management plan. It would be better for bats, however, if they were specifically considered in both cases. Bats should be included in decisions to purchase natural lands. This would include a survey to determine what species of bats are using the land, a listing of the roosting habitat available (palms, hardwoods, Spanish moss, snags, caves, etc.), the types and numbers of foraging areas available (rivers, lakes, streams, ponds, wetlands, prairies, etc.), and some estimate regarding the abundance of bats on the site. If these results are positive, then bat conservation would be one additional justification for the purchase of the land. Likewise, bats should be included as part of a management plan for preserved lands. Primarily, this would consist of protecting the roosting sites and foraging areas on the land, along with a periodic assessment of the status of the bat population.

Preservation of Rural Habitat

In addition to natural lands, bats do well in rural areas where adequate roosting habitat is left undisturbed. Land owners can simply leave palms, hardwoods, Spanish moss, and snags in place to provide bat habitat. Cultivated fields and pastures necessarily displace natural habitat, but tree breaks, clusters of trees in grazing areas, and undisturbed buffer zones can provide important bat habitat for the area. Since a number of the insects eaten by bats are agricultural pests, farmers gain the benefit of additional insect control for essentially no incremental cost. In some areas of the country, farmers have even added bat houses to increase the numbers of bats on their land. Testimonials indicate a significant drop in crop pests as a result. Some bat species will occasionally adopt deserted or rarely used buildings and structures as roosting habitat. Although this is not a proposal to encourage abandoned structures, the lack of disturbance to those that do exist can provide bat habitat as well.

Preservation of Cave Habitat

Caves are a rare and delicate natural resource that demand special care and attention. Because it takes many thousands of years for caves to form, they are considered an irreplaceable natural resource. Caves often contain unique and beautiful mineral formations and provide habitat for rare and endangered plants and animals, many of which can survive only in a cave environment. The very best conservation plan for caves and the biota within them would be to eliminate human disturbance. This is difficult to achieve for several reasons.

Figure 6.2. Snags with loose bark, hollowed areas, and woodpecker cavities often serve as bat roosts (photo by George Marks).

One is that caves are the property of the landowner, and the amount of protection provided is a decision of that owner. For some landowners, a cave on their land is a novelty of unique importance and carefully protected; for others, it simply came with the land and is considered a nuisance and a liability. Secondly, caves, because of their unique characteristics, attract visitors. Some visitors are responsible and careful to prevent damage to the cave or to the life-forms within it. Others fail to understand the destructive consequences of their actions, and a few purposely vandalize the interiors and destroy the wildlife within them. Fortunately, steps have been taken to protect Florida caves. The Florida Cave Protection Act of 1980 (title XLVI, chap. 810, sec. 13 of the Florida Statutes) makes it illegal to vandalize the interior of any Florida cave. This includes defacing the walls or damaging any of the formations. It also makes it illegal to break, force, or tamper with any gates or locks in place to prevent access. It is also illegal to remove, kill, harm, or otherwise disturb any naturally occurring organism within a cave.

Figure 6.3. Florida cave entrance with FWC wildlife biologist (photo by Stan Kirkland/ FWC).

Legal protection, however, is not sufficient. There are many who are not aware of the laws, and some who seem not to care. Caves are often located in remote areas, making enforcement difficult. The entrance to a cave can be gated or the entrance area fenced. At the owner's request, the area can be declared a Critical Wildlife Area and posted accordingly. This gives the Florida Fish and Wildlife Conservation Commission (FWC) the authority to protect the area and enforce the restrictions. In such cases, the FWC and land owner work together for the cave's protection. This is not a proposal to close all caves. It is recognized that a number of Florida caves are valuable for recreational purposes. The Florida Speleological Society has done much to protect and restore Florida caves. This organization educates and trains cavers on how to safely explore caves with minimal or no damage to the interiors or to the biota within them. Some caves, however, are critical to the survival of Florida bat species and need to be protected accordingly. Fortunately, most of these caves are considered of little recreational value. The most successful approach for protecting caves into perpetuity seems to be the purchase of the land by a governmental agency or conservation organization. Once the land is under such ownership, the cave entrance can be gated or fenced and the area posted. In Florida, it has been found that fencing the area surrounding a cave entrance works better than gating the entrance. The entrances to Florida caves are small, and even though gating provides better protection against human intrusion, it often interferes with the bats' use of the cave. In some cases it has caused them to abandon the site.

Preservation of Urban Habitat

Florida bat roost sites have been impacted by urban development in two ways. One, of course, is complete destruction. That is, when areas are developed, trees, both living and dead, are removed and replaced with buildings and roads. Certainly, new trees will be planted, but they will be too low and small to serve as bat roosts for many years. Secondly, even when fully grown trees are present, the Spanish moss will likely be removed, either because it is considered unsightly or the owner erroneously believes it will endanger the tree. Palms will likely be trimmed, eliminating the shag needed to serve as bat roosts. Dead trees will be removed because they are thought to be unsightly or a hazard. Consequently, manmade structures often become the only roost sites available to bats in urban areas.

Bat habitat can be provided in urban areas by allowing fronds to remain on palm trees until they drop naturally, allowing Spanish moss to remain on hardwoods, and where possible, allowing snags to remain standing until they must be removed for safety reasons. Occasionally, clean-up may be required after a windy day when the loose fronds and Spanish moss are blown down, but this is likely less costly than the trimming process. Even a downed snag, however, can be left behind to provide habitat for terrestrial wildlife. This strategy requires public acceptance of the natural beauty of these things, rather than the traditional manicured appearance typical of urban landscapes. The real problem here is not the land or homeowner that chooses to leave things natural; it is the neighbor or homeowner's association that is not willing to accept it. Experience has demonstrated that foliage-roosting bats will return to urban areas where the trees have grown to full size, palm shags are allowed to accumulate, and hardwoods host streamers of Spanish moss. With a little care, a healthy population of bats can coexist in urban areas and join the ranks of songbirds and squirrels as part of our urban wildlife.

Buildings provide attractive roost sites for several Florida bat species. Unfortunately, this often creates problems for the building owners. Improperly conducted bat exclusions or attempted illegal exterminations by building owners often result in the destruction of entire bat colonies and expose the public and pets to poisoned and dying bats. These consequences are unnecessary and avoidable, since there are proven methods for safely evicting bats from buildings. Factors contributing to the general confusion about bats in buildings and the numerous failed attempts at removing them include: owners unaware of

Figure 6.4. Untrimmed dead palm fronds provide habitat in urban environments for Florida's solitary bat species (photo by George Marks).

the available solutions; pest and wildlife control operators not properly trained in the methods; building owners unwilling to pay for a proper solution; a lack of regulations assuring the processes are conducted properly; irresponsible individuals who use scare tactics on building owners for personal gain; and a general false belief that bats are vermin, carry diseases, and are a public health hazard. Obviously, a lot of work is needed in these areas if we are to protect Florida bats.

The addition of bat houses in urban areas can provide bat habitat that is not only beneficial for bats, but also in the public interest. Urban bat houses provide alternative roost sites for bats excluded from buildings and allow bat colonies to remain in the area as a source of natural insect control. They can also be used for educational purposes and as a point of interest for recreational purposes. Two approaches are available. The smaller bat houses can be installed by homeowners in their backyard. The larger community bat houses can be constructed in parks or on unused areas of public facilities. Chapter 8 is dedicated to the construction and location of bat houses.

Bats in Bridges

Some Florida bats are known to adopt bridges as roost sites. Bats are found both in bridges crossing highways and in bridges over water. During 2002–4, the Florida Department of Transportation (FDOT), in conjunction with the Florida Fish and Wildlife Conservation Commission, conducted a study to determine the extent to which bats were occupying bridges, which bridge types were being used, and whether bridges provided safe habitat for bats without posing problems to the public or bridge maintenance personnel. As a result of the study, it was estimated that more than 400 bridges in Florida were being used as bat roosts. Four species of bats were found using bridges: Brazilian free-tailed bats, southeastern myotis, big brown bats, and evening bats. Although not encountered in the study, Rafinesque's big-eared bat had previously been observed using bridges. The bridges most often used were constructed of pre-stressed concrete beams. Bats usually roost in the expansion crevices between bridge sections. Crevices were also used in other bridge types when available, but no bats were found in crevices wider than 2 inches or shallower (crevice depth) than 3 inches. It was also noted that the bats preferred older bridges. There was no evidence of damage to the bridges from the bats, their guano, or their urine. It was also concluded that bats posed little risk to bridge work-

Figure 6.5. Bridge crossing the Suwannee River used as a bat roost site (courtesy of Florida Fish and Wildlife Conservation Commission).

ers or to the public, and a few simple precautions could prevent direct contact with them. It was also recommended that maintenance be scheduled outside of the maternity season, which in Florida runs from mid-April to mid-August. Overall, the study indicated that allowing bats to remain in existing bridges and designing future bridges to be bat-friendly appears to be an easy way of providing additional bat habitat.

A few Florida species have also adopted culverts as roost sites, most notably the southeastern myotis. Culverts offer a safe and secluded area for bats, and the presence of a colony in most cases does not seem to create any problem. Consequently, colonies in culvert roosts should be allowed to remain undisturbed. If it can be determined why particular culverts are attractive to bats, perhaps others could be made more bat-friendly. Two other species have, on occasion, been found in Florida culverts: the big brown bat and Rafinesque's big-eared bat. It may even be possible to install culverts on preserved lands to create artificial roost sites. An artificial culvert roost was constructed in the Lower Suwannee National Wildlife Refuge in 2003 and occasional use by bats was detected by February 2004.

Legal Protection

Bats are classified as Florida wildlife and therefore are protected under Florida's general wildlife laws. The following is an excerpt from chapter 68A-4.001 of the Florida Administrative Code:

> General Prohibitions: No wildlife or freshwater fish or their nests, eggs, young, homes or dens shall be taken, transported, stored, served, bought, sold, or possessed in any manner or quantity at any time except as specifically permitted by these rules nor shall anyone take, poison, store, buy, sell, possess or wantonly or willfully waste the same except as specifically permitted by these rules.

This answers a number of questions that are often asked about bats. Bats cannot be collected from the wild and kept as pets. They cannot be bought or sold as pets. It is illegal to vandalize or disturb colonies of bats. Bats cannot be legally poisoned or exterminated. They can, however, be excluded, provided the exclusion is conducted in a manner that does not wantonly or willfully injure or destroy the bats. Information on how to properly conduct a bat exclusion is provided in chapter 7. Although the administrative code provides legal protection, enforcement and prosecution is often difficult. It is important that the public and conservation organizations help support these laws by informing others of the prohibitions and reporting violations.

A more specific and powerful form of protection is available under the Federal Endangered Species Act of 1973. The U.S. Fish and Wildlife Service (USFWS) oversees this process and determines which species are added and when they are removed. Presently, the gray myotis and the Indiana myotis are the only two Florida species listed as federally endangered. There has been a move to downlist the gray myotis, since the population appears to be stable and all of the known maternity and hibernation caves have been protected. The Indiana myotis is rare in Florida, with only two individuals having ever been found. Cave-dwelling species, such as these, gained early attention in the listing process because they are dependent on limited cave habitat and particularly vulnerable to disturbances. Also, because they roost in caves, their populations are easier to assess and track. Population trends of solitary and foliage-roosting species, on the other hand, are more difficult to determine and, hence, largely unknown. Unless studies can be conducted to prove other species in Florida deserve this form of protection, it provides no help for most of Florida's bats.

At one point, the Florida bonneted bat was considered as a candidate by the USFWS for protection under the Endangered Species Act. However, in 1996 it was dropped from the listing of candidates on the basis of information available at that time indicating the Florida bonneted bat, then known as Wagner's mastiff bat (*Eumops glaucinus floridanus*), was a subspecies of the larger population of *Eumops glaucinus* found throughout much of Central and South America and the Greater Antilles. A recent study conducted by Robert Timm and Hugh Genoways, however, concluded that the Florida bonneted bat is actually a separate species. It has now been reclassified as *Eumops floridanus*. This means it is a bat species endemic to Florida, with a small population and a very limited range. In the closing lines of their paper Timm and Genoways state that "the Florida bonneted bat is one of the most critically endangered mammal species in North America." Steps need to be taken to have the USFWS once again consider this species for protection under the Endangered Species Act.

In addition to the federal listing, the State of Florida manages a listing of imperiled Florida species. The Florida Fish and Wildlife Conservation Commission is responsible for the management of this list. The listing classifies imperiled species as Endangered, Threatened, or Species of Special Concern. Chapter 68A-27 of the Florida Administrative Code defines the protections afforded each classification and the process for adding or removing species from the list. The code specifies that it is illegal to kill, attempt to kill, wound, pursue, molest, harm, harass, capture, possess, or sell any species listed as Endangered. The provisions for Threatened and Species of Special Concern are only slightly less restrictive. The listing currently includes the gray myotis, the Indiana myotis, and the Florida bonneted bat as Endangered.

A major problem complicating bat conservation is that bats frequently adopt buildings as roost sites. Many building owners are unaware that bats are protected under Florida wildlife laws and attempt to exterminate them, seal the entrances, or use various other methods resulting in unnecessary bat mortality. Chapter 68A-12.009 of the Florida Administrative Code specifies what property owners can and cannot do when wildlife impacts their property, but there is no specific wording regarding bats. This has resulted in confusion and frustration for building owners and conservationists alike. The most likely reasons for no specific wording on bats are the past lack of concern, and the unavailability of published information on how to properly exclude bats from buildings. Over the past decade, methods have been developed for conducting successful bat exclusions (chapter 7), a process that allows bats to exit but not re-enter a roost. Administrative rules need to be written that permit successful exclusion methods and disallow methods and timing known to cause bat mortality.

Rescue and Rehabilitation

Wildlife mortality is expected in a natural ecosystem as a result of predation, natural disasters, and changes in the abundance of food resources. So, one might ask, why should we be concerned about the death of a bat? Saving one injured or orphaned bat, or even a hundred, will likely not noticeably affect the overall population, but there are some very good reasons for doing so. In most cases, bats brought into rehabilitation centers have been injured or orphaned as a result of human causes. The negative impacts of human expansion on the natural flora and fauna of Florida is undeniable. We have a responsibility to care for what we have so adversely impacted. By caring for injured and orphaned wildlife, rehabilitators are sending a message to the community that wildlife is important. Many rehabilitators provide educational programs and are activists supporting the protection of wildlife. Additionally, rehabilitators who work with bats learn about the species in the area, their relative health, behaviors, and reproduction. This information can be useful in the conservation of native bat populations. All of the above taken together make rehabilitation an important part of bat conservation.

Fortunately, there are a number of qualified wildlife rehabilitators in the state of Florida. If you need to locate a wildlife rehabilitator in your area, you can contact the Florida Fish and Wildlife Conservation Commission, the governing body that licenses wildlife rehabilitators in Florida. If you are specifically looking for someone who will accept injured or orphaned bats, you can contact the Florida Bat Conservancy (FBC). The FBC maintains a list of rehabilitators who work with bats in Florida, many of whom are members of the Florida Wildlife

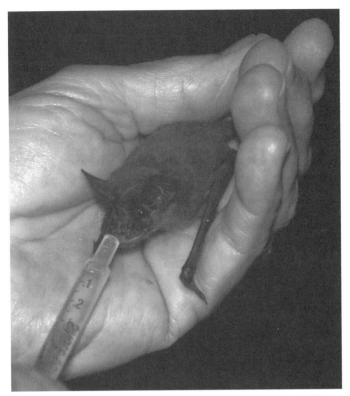

Figure 6.6. Brazilian free-tailed bat being offered water by wildlife rehabilitator (photo by George Marks).

Rehabilitators Association (FWRA). Members of the FWRA network to share information on rehabilitation methods and to provide mutual assistance in caring for Florida wildlife. Experience and knowledge regarding the care of injured and orphaned bats has expanded considerably over the past decade, thanks to dedicated workers who have not only cared for bats but also taken the time to document the methods and share them with others.

Research

One of the keys to conservation is knowing the current status and population trend of a species. Unfortunately, little is known about the abundance and population trends of most Florida bats. Without being able to make definitive statements, it is difficult to justify protection, even though a species may be in peril. Consequently, population assessments of species whose numbers are suspected to be low or declining should be a first priority.

Figure 6.7. Bat researchers taking measurements (photo by George Marks).

Much of what we know about the diets of Florida bats is based on studies of these same species elsewhere in the United States. Studies are needed to specifically identify what insects are being eaten by bats in Florida. For example, are they important consumers of agricultural pests? If so, this knowledge would be helpful in gaining support for the protection of Florida bats. It would also reveal which insects are important for their survival. On a related topic, it would be important to know the impact of pesticides on Florida's bat populations. Such control certainly reduces the quantity of insects in an area. What is the resulting impact on bat populations? If bats are foraging in an area recently sprayed with insecticides, does ingesting the insects impact the health of the bats?

Although bat houses in Florida are becoming more successful, could research projects develop even better designs for Florida's climate and bat species? Is a bat house specifically designed for a given species more successful than a generic one? Would some species of bats choose to move into a masonry design over a wooden design? Bat houses today are designed primarily for bats that will move into manmade structures. Is it possible to construct successful artificial roosts for foliage-roosting species? Can culverts and bridges be better designed to serve as bat roosts?

One of the consequences resulting from the general misconceptions about bats is that they are among the last mammals to be considered for conservation. Because they are difficult to study, they are also among the last mammals for which scientific data have been accumulated regarding their status and needs. Public sentiment is changing, and interest in conducting bat research is increasing. It is important that these trends be channeled to expedite the bat conservation measures needed in Florida and move us beyond the "catch-up" mode.

7

Bats in Buildings

Many people are shocked when they discover that a colony of bats has moved into their home. They wonder why they have been singled out for what they believe to be a rare and catastrophic occurrence. Usually, they have no idea how to solve the problem and frantically search the Yellow Pages, surf the Internet, and ask friends and neighbors for advice. They are shocked once again to discover a wide range of conflicting information about bats in buildings and extreme differences in the proposed methods for removing them. Additionally, they may encounter scare tactics and be told horror stories about rabies, histoplasmosis, and parasites. Attempts may be made to remove the bats using incorrect methods, creating even more problems for the owner, not to mention the bats. Actually, bats frequently occur in buildings, and their presence is certainly not a cause for panic. In this chapter, we will address why bats move into buildings, how a stray bat can be removed from a room, and how colonies of bats can be safely excluded from a building.

Why Bats Move into Buildings

Bats that will move into buildings are primarily colonial species that, in the wild, would roost in old dead trees, caves, and cliff crevices. There are very few cliffs in Florida, and caves suitable for bats are scarce and found only in the northern portion of the state. Dead trees, however, were part of the natural landscape throughout most of Florida for thousands of years. As urbanization expanded, dead trees were eliminated and buildings erected in their place. This both destroyed and created bat habitat. In many ways, wooden structures are like dead trees, and concrete structures are like caves and cliffs. Colonial bats prefer warm, secluded locations that are safe from predators, protected from the weather, and that, during the maternity season, provide an environment suitable for rearing young. The small openings leading into eaves and attics, and the small crevices in many concrete structures provide, at least from the bat's point of view, an acceptable alternative to its natural roosting habitat.

Bats do not chew or gnaw their way into structures. They are not like rodents and do not have the teeth for the job. The only way a bat can enter a building

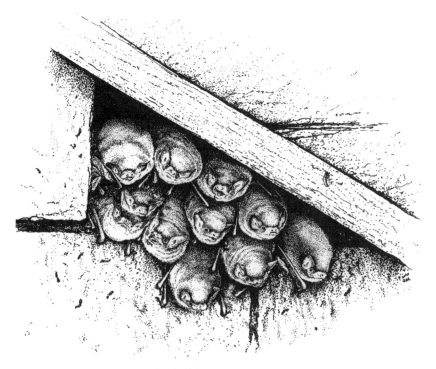

Figure 7.1. Bats roosting inside a building.

is through an already existing opening. There are many parts of a building that may have areas where bats can enter. Some of these are due to the design of the building, some to construction methods, and some to building deterioration. Common entrance points include: gaps created where fascia boards overlap uneven surfaces; gaps behind flashing, especially along the edge of flat roofs; and areas where different construction elements meet, such as where a projecting gabled section joins the roofline. As a building ages, deteriorating screens behind louvered attic vents or under soffits can provide entrances. Sometimes squirrels, woodpeckers, rats, or other animals create openings later used by bats. A walk around a building once or twice a year to look for any location where age has caused building materials to warp, crack, or move and create openings is well worth the few minutes it takes to do it. When inspecting a two-story building, binoculars can be helpful, as small openings may otherwise not be visible from the ground. If you see an opening that appears large enough to insert your thumb, bats will be able to use it as an entrance.

There are some building areas where bats can roost but are unable to gain access into the building. Tile roofs are a prime example. Barrel tile roofs are popular in Florida, and older styles offer numerous gaps and crevices attractive to bats. Large colonies can take up residence in such a roof. The small weep-holes at the end of the tile rows are not of concern because they are usually too small for bats to use, but poorly fitting eave-closures and roof edges, where tiles overlap fascia boards, can provide easy access. Fortunately, when bats are roosting under roof tiles, there is usually no way the bats can enter the building. Bats can also roost behind window shutters, or commercial signs attached to buildings, but these do not allow access into the building. Decorative facades and mansards are also attractive to bats as roost sites. In these cases, the possibility of bats accessing the interior of the building depends on how carefully the building was constructed and sealed.

Removing a Bat from a Room

A stray bat will occasionally find its way into the living quarters of a building. The most common reason is that someone has sealed an exterior opening that a colony of bats was using as an emergence point. Sometimes this is done unknowingly during renovations, or while caulking in preparation for painting. It also happens when people, in an attempt to evict bats, plug holes at night, believing that all the bats have left the roost. Bats that have been sealed into a building will, in desperation, search for another exit and one or more may find an opening into the interior areas. During the maternity season, while mother bats are away from the roost foraging, young bats may stray from the roost, ending up where they do not belong. If bats are consistently entering the interior portion of a building, look carefully for holes in the walls or ceiling that are allowing access. In particular, check for gaps around electrical wires or water pipes, or the holes behind appliances, and seal them as necessary. Hardware cloth can be placed behind the air-conditioning vents in a room to make sure bats are not entering through deteriorated air-conditioning ductwork in the attic. A less common occurrence is a bat flying in through a door or window left open after dark.

Upon discovering a bat in a room, the first step is to remain calm. The bat will not attempt to attack people, but it may be frantically flying about, trying to find an exit. A bat trapped in a room will often fly from one side of the room to the other in a swooping pattern. If you are in the middle of the room, it may appear as if the bat is trying to attack you. So, it is best to stand to the side, out of the way. A few minutes spent watching the bat's behavior can help determine the best method for capturing it, or getting it to leave through an exit. If the room is dark, turn on a light so you can adequately see what the bat is doing. The light will not bother the bat. If you turn out the lights, you may lose track of the bat and not know whether it has left, or if it is hiding somewhere in the room. If there are any exterior doors, or windows (without screens), open them and give the bat a chance to find its own way out. If the bat is clinging to a wall and not flying after you open the doors or windows, allow it a little time. The bat will likely detect the open door or window using its eyesight or echolocation, or by sensing the air current, and quickly exit once it starts flying again.

If there are no convenient exterior doors or windows, or if the bat refuses to fly, you can carefully capture it. If the bat is active, this may take some time and patience. If it has been trapped inside for several days, it may be weak and easy to catch. If you have encountered the bat at rest during the daytime, it may be in torpor and will be easy to capture. Bats grip onto surfaces using the tiny claws on their toes and thumbs, so care must be taken not to injure them. The best tool for this job is a clear plastic container so you can see the bat, but a box, can, or similar container will also work. Slowly approach the bat and place the container over it (figure 7.2). If disturbed, the bat may take flight, but a bat that has been at rest for a while will usually remain still while you do this. Slip a piece of cardboard between the container and the wall or floor, being careful to allow the bat to move its feet and wings out of the way. If a container is not available, or if the bat has roosted on an uneven surface, such as a curtain, you can use a thick towel to capture it. Slowly approach the bat. Place the towel over it and gently scoop it up, wrapping the towel around it as you lift it off the surface. If done slowly, the bat will normally release its toes and thumbs from the surface and grip onto the towel. Another approach is to use heavy leather work gloves. Cloth gloves are not recommended since the bat, if frightened, could bite through them. This method has a higher chance of harming the bat, because in attempting to keep it secure, it may be handled roughly or grabbed too tightly. Approach the bat and place your gloved hands over the top of it. Then wrap one gloved hand around and behind the bat, allowing it to transfer its grip from the surface to the glove.

Attempting to capture a bat while flying is not recommended because it is very difficult to do, even with something like a large butterfly net. The violent nature of this approach is likely to injure the bat or damage the appointments in the room. If you do have an appropriate net and attempt this, the best approach is to capture the bat from behind as it flies by. The bat's senses and agility are such that safely capturing it from the front is nearly impossible. Continued attempts will panic the bat further and stress it unnecessarily.

If anyone was bitten or suspected of being bitten by the bat, *do not release it*. Call the local health department or animal control office. They will arrange to have the bat tested for rabies. Only a small percentage of bats contract rabies, but you cannot afford to take the chance. If the bat tests positive, anyone bitten

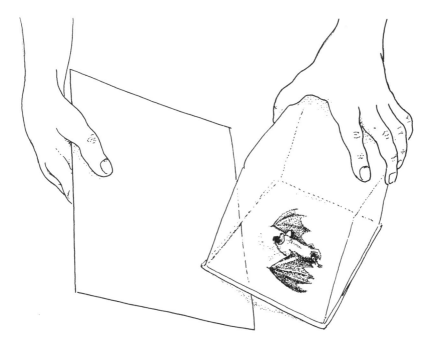

Figure 7.2. Removing a bat using a container.

will need to be vaccinated promptly to protect them from the disease. Anyone who came into physical contact with the bat should contact their local health department or medical practitioner to determine if they should be vaccinated.

If no one was bitten, the bat can simply be released outside. If you have captured the bat in a container, hold the container up high and tilt the opening slightly downward, allowing the bat to move to the edge of the container and take flight when it is ready. Do not simply leave the container outside at night in an upright position. Bats have difficulty flying up and out of a container, so it should be positioned such that the bat can crawl to the edge and drop out. If it has been captured in a towel, the towel can be held high, allowing the bat to take flight, or it can be hung on a bush, tree limb, fence, or other structure. If the bat has been captured using gloves, you can gently transfer it to the trunk of a tree, or to a place where it can hang until it is ready to fly. It may take the bat several minutes to orient itself before taking flight. A flashlight is useful during a release because when the bat drops to take flight, it may appear to have fallen onto the ground. If you are not sure whether the bat has become airborne successfully, you can use the flashlight to check the ground around you. Bats should not be released during the daytime because they probably will not fly and will be exposed to predators if left in the open. If the bat was captured during the daytime, it can be kept in a container until evening. The best time for releasing a bat is at emergence time (15–20 minutes after sunset). This is the natural time for them to have their heart rate and body temperature up and be ready for flight.

If the bat is injured, appears weak, or refuses to fly, place it in a cardboard box or container. Include a cloth (t-shirts work well) or small towel. The bat will settle down and feel more secure if it can cling to the fabric and hide within its folds. A little water can be added in a jar lid or similar container, but do not try to feed it. Most of Florida's bats capture insects in flight and will not recognize insects placed in a box as food. Attempting to hand-feed insects or other foods to the bat may result in getting bitten. Close the lid and make sure there are openings for air. Place the box in a safe location and out of direct sunlight. Contact a local wildlife rehabilitator and offer to drop it off at their location or meet them halfway. If you need help finding a rehabilitator in your area, you can contact the Florida Bat Conservancy or the Florida Fish and Wildlife Conservation Commission.

Bat Colonies in Buildings

Sometimes bats roost in areas of buildings or under tile roofs where they don't cause any problems. A small colony of bats may go unnoticed for years. Often it is a neighbor who first notices bats emerging in the evening or re-entering just before dawn. If bats become a nuisance for a home or building owner, a bat "exclusion" is the only safe and successful method of removal. An exclusion is a method of evicting bats by positioning one-way devices at the emergence points of the roost. This allows the bats to exit naturally but prevents re-entry. Physically capturing a colony within the roost and relocating it is almost never successful because the bats are usually tucked into areas of the building that are not accessible. Even if bats are in an open area, attempts to capture them will likely cause them to flee to inaccessible areas. If bats are captured and released elsewhere, they will attempt to return to their original roost, often flying long distances if necessary.

Do not attempt to poison or exterminate bats. The use of poisons or fumigants on bats is illegal in the United States, and violates the Federal Insecticide, Fungicide, and Rodenticide Act. In addition to being illegal, the use of poisons to kill bats creates more problems than it solves. Dead bats scattered throughout an attic, or piles of decaying bodies in the walls or ceilings of a building, will attract insects and create a foul and probably unbearable odor. Attempts to poison bats may also result in sick and dying bats wandering into the living quarters of the building or ending up on the ground in the surrounding neighborhood.

Figure 7.3. Bat emerging from beneath a roof tile (photo by George Marks).

This greatly increases the risk of people and pets encountering dead and dying bats. A situation like this can become a nightmare for public health officials who must determine if any exposures to rabies have occurred.

Don't just plug the holes. Many people are under the impression that they can patch the holes at midnight while the bats are gone. Unfortunately, not every bat leaves the roost every night. Temperature, insect availability, and other factors determine whether bats leave, and when they return. Some bats may forage for an hour or so during the early evening, then return to the roost and forage again in the early morning just before sunrise. Sealing a hole during the night will most likely cause bats to be trapped inside.

Do not conduct a bat exclusion during the maternity season. In Florida, exclusions should not be conducted from mid-April through mid-August. This is when mother bats are giving birth and rearing their young. Performing exclusions during this time of year will create major problems for both the bats and the building owner. During the early part of the maternity season, the mother bats leave their young inside while they forage for insects. An exclusion at this time will result in the young bats being trapped inside without their mothers and dying of starvation and dehydration. During the latter part of the maternity season, the young leave with the mothers and learn how to forage, use their echolocation, and capture insects on their own. The mothers supplement their diet with milk until the young can sufficiently sustain themselves. Performing an exclusion at this time will disrupt this process, resulting in unnecessary juvenile mortality.

The situation is more complex in the extreme southern portion of the state and the Florida Keys. Two of Florida's resident species, the velvety free-tailed bat and the Florida bonneted bat, are polyestrous; that is, births can occur at more than one time during the year. The Florida bonneted bat, a unique species to Florida, is so rare that the timing of births, and hence the proper timing of exclusions, has not been fully studied. Although the velvety free-tailed bat has been studied in Cuba, it has only recently become colonized in Florida, and the safe timing for exclusions has not been determined. Field studies of these two species need to be conducted to understand their maternity cycles and define in which months exclusions can be conducted without risking infant or juvenile mortality. If an exclusion is to be conducted in a building serving as a roost for one of these species, it is recommended that the Florida Fish and Wildlife Conservation Commission be contacted for advice before proceeding.

Conducting a Bat Exclusion

Exclusion techniques have been developed over the years and, when properly applied, are almost always successful on the first attempt. If an entrance point is missed, an exclusion can be reconducted for that area. The following steps will both explain the process and provide a checklist for conducting an exclusion.

Step 1. *Find the entry points.* This can be done by observing the building during emergence time. Bats typically emerge from their roost about 15–20 minutes after sunset, but it is best to start watching at sunset to be sure you don't miss any. If temperatures are chilly, bats may not emerge, so warmer nights are best. If there are multiple emergence points, try to position yourself at a corner where you can observe two sides of the building at the same time. Another person may be positioned to watch the other sides of the building. An emergence may happen quickly, especially if the colony is small. The areas you should be watching carefully are the edges of the roof, eaves and soffits, and any other feature of the house that may have gaps allowing bats to enter. A closer look at a hole or crevice that bats are using will probably reveal some staining around it from their body oils, and a scattering of bat droppings on the wall.

Step 2. *Bat-proof all other openings.* Carefully survey the exterior of the building during the daytime. Now that you have observed the emergence and know what holes or crevices the bats are using, you can seal up any other holes that may get used once the exclusion begins. After being excluded, the bats will be frantically looking for any other way to get back into the building. If they find another opening, the exclusion process will need to be repeated in that area. Most openings can be repaired by replacing loose or rotted building material or screens. There are a number of caulking products that can be used to fill holes. Keep in mind that some bats can enter a crevice as small as ½ inch, or a hole as small as ¾ inch in diameter. Temporary fixes may be achieved by attaching ¼-inch hardware cloth over the opening until a permanent solution can be put in place.

Step 3. *Install exclusion devices.* An exclusion device allows the bats to exit the opening unharmed, but prevents them from re-entering. Several exclusion methods have been developed over the years. The preferred method is to use an industrial quality bird netting. A known supplier is InterNet, Inc., Minneapolis, Minnesota. Although many large hardware and gardening supply stores sell bird netting, the larger weave and lighter weight of these products will often entangle the bats. Netting with ¼-inch mesh works best. Bats may be able to get through a larger mesh size or become entangled while trying. Smaller mesh sizes may enable bats to land on the netting and easily crawl around on it, possibly reentering the roost.

To conduct the exclusion, attach the netting above the opening using staples, Velcro tabs, or duct tape. The netting should extend below the hole or crevice about 12 inches. The sides of the netting should be attached in a way that creates space over the opening for the bats to exit and fly out the bottom (figure 7.4). If you can easily slide your hand up under the netting, it should provide sufficient space for the bats to exit freely. When the bats return, they will attempt to fly directly to the hole or crevice, but it will be blocked by the netting. They will not land on the wall below the netting and climb up behind it to reach the hole. Although the bottom edge remains open, the netting must be well-secured at the top and on both sides.

Almost every situation is a little different. Observing how bats normally leave and re-enter a roost may help you determine the best way to position the netting and give you a better understanding of the process. The exclusion netting can

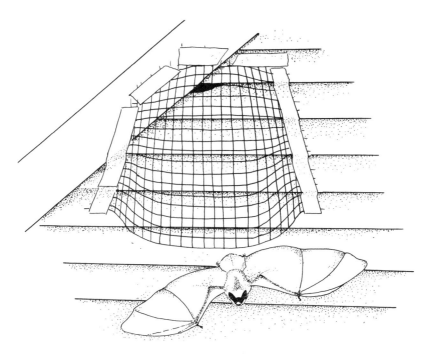

Figure 7.4. Use of exclusion netting.

then be attached during the day when there is plenty of light. It is a good idea to watch the emergence the first night after the exclusion system is up to make sure it is working properly and that bats are not getting trapped behind the netting. If a bat becomes tangled in the netting, remove it carefully while wearing heavy leather work gloves.

When the opening is a hole underneath a ceiling or eave, or away from walls, plastic sleeves can be designed to effect the exclusion. Exclusion sleeves can be made by taking a sheet of plastic, cutting a 2- to 3-foot length, rolling it, and using duct tape, creating a tube or chute (figure 7.5). Two-inch slits can be cut in one end to form tabs that can be taped or stapled to the ceiling. The bats will drop down the tube, and the slick surface of the plastic will prevent re-entry. The diameter of the tube should be about eight inches, but can be made larger if necessary. Devices such as these are referred to as "excluders." PVC pipe, with a two-inch or wider diameter, can also be used, but is a little more difficult to fasten because of its weight. Care must be taken when using PVC pipe that it does not protrude into the roost area in such a way that prevents the bats from exiting through it.

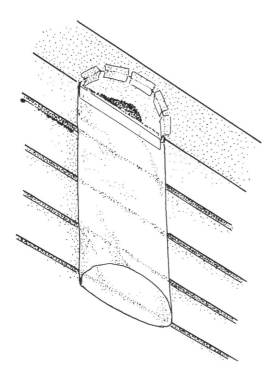

Figure 7.5. Use of a plastic
sleeve as an exclusion device.

It is important to install exclusion devices at all emergence points. If a few emergence points are close together (within a few feet) and it is known there is nothing preventing the bats from moving from one point to the other inside the structure, it may be possible to seal some and exclude others. If the distance between the emergence points is significant, or if it cannot be assured there is easy passage internally from one area to the other, each should be provided with a separate excluder. Attempting to seal emergence points to reduce the number of excluders for a large area can result in bats entering the living quarters of the building in search of an exit, or worse, failing to find one at all.

Step 4. *Allow time for the bats to leave.* Before removing the netting, observe the area carefully at emergence time to make sure no more bats are exiting. It usually takes at least three to four clear, warm nights for all of the bats to leave. Bats tend not to forage on cold or rainy nights, so if the weather turns bad it will be necessary to extend the exclusion. When conducting an exclusion during the winter, the netting may need to be left up much longer, particularly in north Florida. If bats are still coming out, then they have either found another way back in, or the exclusion system is not working and needs to be revised. If the exclusion materials become loose or detached, the bats will be able to re-enter, so make sure it remains secure throughout the process. Bats will be checking continually to see if they can re-enter their roost.

Step 5. *Permanently seal the openings.* After the bats have been successfully excluded, the netting or exclusion device can be removed during the daytime and the opening permanently sealed. Do not leave the netting down without sealing the opening, or the bats will move back in the following night. If the opening cannot be sealed immediately, the exclusion devices may be left up longer, but there is a risk that wind, storms, or failure of fasteners could allow the bats to re-enter. Another approach is to take the netting down and effect a temporary patch until the opening can be permanently sealed.

Step 6. *Cleanup.* If a colony of bats has been in a roost for a long time, there may be an odor and an accumulation of guano inside the roost area. In most cases, the odor is actually from the scent gland, not the guano, of Brazilian free-tailed bats, a common building-occupant in Florida. This odor should disperse shortly after the bats are gone. Bat guano consists of tiny particles of chewed up insects, and can usually be left undisturbed if it is in dry areas of the building that are not used, or are inaccessible. Although the fungus responsible for histoplasmosis can grow in bat droppings, the environmental conditions must be right for it to survive (chapter 9). The attic areas of buildings are usually dry, and not conducive to growth of the fungus. To date, the fungus has not been found in a building in Florida as a result of bat guano.

Other Methods

Other methods have been used to remove bats from buildings, but they are usually unsuccessful or, at best, only partially successful. Naphthalene, the chemical ingredient in moth balls, has often been used for repelling bats. It is the only chemical registered for use as a repellent for bat roosts. While naphthalene may chase bats away for a while, they will often return as the odor fades. Because large amounts of naphthalene are needed to effectively repel a bat colony, it could possibly pose a health risk for the building occupants, not to mention subject them to the unpleasant odor. Bright lights have occasionally been used to force bats to leave an area or prevent them from using it as a roost. This is not always successful, but it may be the only option available for an area that is difficult to seal, such as a large open warehouse or barn. The lights need to be positioned to eliminate dark or shadowed areas that could serve as bat roosts. Care must be taken in locating the lamps and wiring to prevent a fire hazard. From time to time, ultrasonic sound-generating devices have been promoted as a means of eliminating bats from buildings. Studies and reported experiences have indicated that these devices are not effective.

～

When bats are excluded, colonies are forced to find new roost sites, which are usually other buildings in the same area. They then become a problem for the next home or business owner who must now exclude them from their new roost. This process continues, creating cost and frustration for property owners as bats are chased from one building to another or, worse, illegally exterminated. The problem can be prevented by bat-proofing buildings before bats move in. Buildings should be designed without exterior features attractive to bats as roost sites, and the construction should be carefully conducted to eliminate unintended voids and openings that would enable bats to gain entry.

8

Bat Houses

A bat house is a great way to encourage bats to take up residence in your area. At first, bat houses were not very successful and people became discouraged, but much has been learned over the past decade. Bat Conservation International (BCI), based in Austin, Texas, has conducted considerable research on the topic and now provides a wealth of helpful information to the general public. The success of the University of Florida bat house in Gainesville has also yielded useful information on bat house design. Discussions with bat house owners all over Florida have yielded useful insights and information, as well. Based on what has been learned, we can offer guidelines and suggestions regarding bat houses in Florida that will significantly increase the chances of success. Because bats are wild animals (and we like it that way), we cannot control what they do. No method has been found for attracting bats to a bat house, although a number of things have been tried. Experience has shown it is not possible to successfully move a colony of bats into a bat house. They simply abandon it and return to the area from which they came. The best we can do is design and locate a bat house in a way that meets their needs, and wait patiently for them to find it and move in.

Bat House Design

Many bat house designs have been tried. Over a period of years these designs have converged into what might be referred to as the traditional backyard bat house. Although there is room for more experimentation, this design has developed a successful track record. Plans for this design are included in this chapter. It is essentially a boxlike structure with a roof but no floor. The open bottom permits entrance and egress of the bats and allows the guano to fall to the ground. There is a 4–6-inch area at the bottom of the bat house, appropriately referred to as the "landing pad," for the bats to land on and crawl up into the house. The species of bats that would normally move into a bat house are gregarious by nature and like to squeeze closely together into tight crevices. Consequently, inside the bat house there may be one or more partitions (dividers). The spaces between the partitions provide crevices where the bats can

Figure 8.1. This backyard bat house has served as a roost for both Brazilian free-tailed bats and Florida bonneted bats (photo by George Marks).

cluster close together. Each crevice is also referred to as a "chamber," so a bat house with two partitions would be referred to as a triple-chambered bat house. A bat house with no partitions would be referred to as a single-chambered bat house. Bat house designs in Florida with ¾-inch crevices have proven quite successful.

It is also important that the surface on at least one side of each crevice be sufficiently rough for bats to grip with their hind claws. The simplest approach is to use rough lumber. If the lumber is smooth-surfaced, horizontal grooves can be cut about ½ inch apart. Another approach is to staple ⅛- to ¼-inch heavy-duty

Table 8.1. Bat House Candidates by Geographic Region

Common Name	Northwest	North	Central	South	Keys
Big brown bat	P	P	P	P	—
Brazilian free-tailed bat	C	C	C	C	—
Evening bat	C	C	C	C	—
Florida bonneted bat	—	—	—	P	—
Southeastern myotis	P	P	P	—	—
Velvety free-tailed bat	—	—	—	—	P

Note: C = Common, P = Possible, — = Not expected or never recorded.

plastic mesh to the wood on one side of each crevice. An alternative is to use plastic window screen. Plastic window screen, however, does not last as long, and buckles with time, reducing the amount of available space within the bat house. If using a thick mesh, you may want to increase the crevice size slightly so the crevice width is not reduced to less than ¾ inch.

Although crevice size seems to be the most critical design factor, a couple of other parameters are important as well. One is the overall size of the bat house. The bigger the bat house, the more likely it is to become occupied. It is also important for the bat house to be sufficiently tall that the bats can move up and down inside as the temperature changes throughout the day. A tall bat house will tend to be warmer at the top and cooler at the bottom. These factors, along with personal experience, suggest that a bat house should be at least 24 inches tall and 12 inches wide. The depth is a function of the number of chambers and the width of the crevices. Another way of enhancing the temperature differential inside the house is to locate a vent about a third of the way up from the bottom. This provides additional cooling in the lower region of the bat house.

If you are going to put up a bat house, it is helpful to know what species of bats might move into it. Not all bats will move into a bat house. The bats that normally move into a bat house are colonial bats. Solitary-roosting bats seldom, if ever, move into a bat house. Furthermore, you will be selecting or building a bat house for the bats that normally reside in your geographic area. Table 8.1 lists the species most likely to move into a bat house for various regions within Florida.

For most bats in Florida, the traditional bat house design with ¾-inch crevices works well. Evening bats, Brazilian free-tailed bats, and southeastern myotis seem to prefer the smaller crevices. Big brown bats are not as common in Florida, but if you wish to include them as candidates for your bat house, you may want to provide crevice widths of up to one inch. If you live in south Florida, you have the opportunity of providing habitat for the endangered Florida bonneted bat. For this much larger bat, you will want to include crevices of up to 1¾ inches. A variety of crevices can be offered by building a bat house with two or three different crevice sizes, or by installing both a single-chambered bat house (which has a larger interior size) and a multichambered bat house back-to-back on the same post, or side-by-side on a building.

Bat House Construction

If you decide to build your own bat house, there are a few other important considerations. First is the type of wood used for construction. Most woods will work, but some are more durable than others. There are bat house builders who feel it would be best to avoid strongly scented woods, such as cedar, but there has been no proof that this is a problem. It is best to avoid pressure-treated lumber for the bat house because of the chemicals used in the process, but pressure-treated lumber is recommended for the post or supports. Exterior-grade plywood works well as long as the edges exposed to the weather are sealed or painted. Actually, the best choice would be lumber from an old building. Bat houses often need to age before bats move in, and aged lumber may accelerate the process. A second consideration is the hardware used in construction. Wood screws have proven superior to nails. Nails tend to pull out as exposed wood warps in the sun. Make sure screws and fasteners are designed for exterior use. The roof should be watertight, with caulking applied as necessary. Since the roof will be exposed to direct sunlight, you may wish to cover it with roofing material. The third consideration is paint. Although it is often recommended that bat houses be painted a dark color in northern states to increase heat absorption, it is not necessary to paint a bat house for this purpose in Florida. Painting a bat house will, however, greatly extend its life. If you choose to paint the bat house, a medium shade of brown or gray is probably best in Florida. Painting a bat house black in Florida could actually make it too hot. If you are mounting a bat house on a building, there appears to be no problem, at least in Florida, with painting it a compatible color. We know of a number of successful bat houses painted in this way.

Choosing a Location

There is no known way of attracting bats to a bat house. Many things have been tried. For example, bat guano has been placed inside bat houses, the wood from old bat roosts has been used to build new ones, and recordings of bats chattering in their roost have been played repeatedly. None of these methods seem to make a noticeable difference in attracting bats. It appears that the bats need to discover the bat house on their own, check it out, and move in. So, as a new

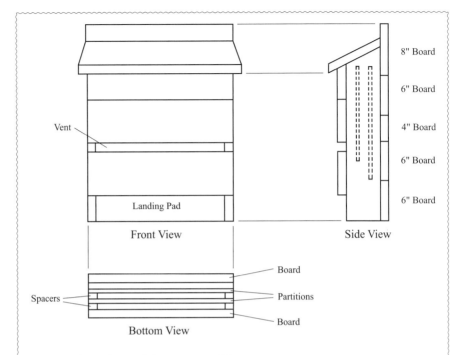

Vent

Landing Pad

Front View

8" Board

6" Board

4" Board

6" Board

6" Board

Side View

Board

Spacers

Partitions

Board

Bottom View

Triple-chambered Bat House Plans

Materials

One 1" × 8" (7¼") board, 3 feet long
One 1" × 6" (5½") board, 8 feet long
One 1" × 4" (3½") board, 6 feet long
Two 1" × 1" (¾") boards, each 3 feet long
One 4' × 4' sheet of ¼" exterior grade plywood
One 4' × 4' sheet of plastic mesh (preferred) or plastic window screen
Six 1¼" #6 galvanized or stainless steel wood screws
Forty 1½" #8 galvanized or stainless steel wood screws
Note: Parentheses indicate expected actual size.

Instructions

Step 1

From the 1×6, cut six 14" sections for the front and back panels of the bat house.

From the 1×8, cut one 16" section for the roof and one 14" section for the back.

From the 1×1s, cut four 17" sections. These will be used as spacers to secure the partitions.

From the 1×4, cut one additional 14" section for the back.

From the remaining piece of the 1×4, cut two sections for the sides. One end of each piece will be cut at a 30-degree angle for the roof. This can be done by cutting each piece with a front length of 21½" and a back length of 23½".

From the plywood sheet, cut a 17" × 12½" section for the back partition, and a 16" × 12½" section for the front partition.

You can check your cuts by temporarily assembling the bat house on its back without glue or fasteners.

Step 2

Bevel the back of the 16" roof section at 30 degrees. The roof will look best if the top (widest side) is made 6½" wide when the bevel is cut. Bevel the long edge of one of the 14" × 6" pieces at 30 degrees. This piece will be used at the top of the front and the bevel is necessary to match the roof.

Step 3

Begin assembly of the bat house by placing the two side pieces on a table with the long sides up and 14" apart. It is recommended that glue or caulking be used as the bat house is assembled to strengthen and weatherproof it. Place one of the 14" × 6" pieces on top and align it with the bottom of the two side pieces. Fasten it with two 1½" wood screws on each side. Repeat the process with a 6", 4", 6", and 8" piece, in that order. This will place the 8" piece at the top of the bat house.

Step 4

Cut a section of screen 14" wide × 29" long (or mesh 12½" wide × 23" long). Place it on the back wall of the bat house. If using screen, fold about 4½" under at the bottom to provide double thickness for the landing pad and fold about an inch over at the top to provide rigidity. Fasten the screen or mesh in place using a 1×1 in the left- and right-hand corners on each side. Secure the 1×1 to the back wall, with the bottom ends located 4½" from the bottom of the bat house. This will create a 4½" landing pad. Use three 1¼" wood screws in each; one in the center and the other two about ¾" from each end. Make sure the top wood screw securely attaches the 1×1 to the 8" board on the back wall. This will add strength to the bat house. Staple the screen or mesh to the back with vertical rows of staples at 2– to 3–inch intervals to keep it from buckling.

Step 5

If using plastic window screen, cut two sections of screen 14" wide × 19" long. Place a plywood partition on top of each, and wrap the edges of the screen over it. It is best to cut notches in the corners so they will fold over flat. Staple the folded-over portion of the screen to the plywood using ¼" staples. If plastic mesh is used, it can be cut to the same dimensions as the partitions. Use ¼" staples so they do not protrude through the partition. Staple vertical rows as before to prevent buckling.

Step 6

Place the 17" partition on top of the two 1×1 pieces already fastened to the back of the bat house, with the screen-covered side up. Place the remaining two 1×1 pieces on each side of it and align them to be directly above the previous two. Place the 16" partition on top (screen-covered side up). Align at the top, allowing 1" of the 1×1 pieces to show at the bottom. This open space makes it easier for bats to crawl into the forward crevices. Now, fasten the two plywood sections and associated 1×1 pieces using two 1½" screws on each side. Locate them about 1½" from the top and bottom of the plywood partition to avoid the screws beneath.

Step 7

Place the beveled 14" × 6" board at the top of the front, aligning the beveled edge with the 30-degree angle of the two side pieces. Fasten it using two 1½" screws on each side. Repeat using a second 14" × 6" board. Locate the third and final 14" × 6" board about ½" down from the previous one to form the ½" gap for the vent.

Step 8

Center the roof section with the beveled edge against the back wall, such that there is equal overhang on each side. Fasten it to the side pieces using two 1½" screws. The roof should be caulked where it meets the back wall. Roofing material can be added if desired. It is recommended that the bat house be painted to extend its life. A brown color works well in Florida.

Step 9

Drill one ⁵⁄₁₆" hole at the top, and one ⁵⁄₁₆" hole at the bottom. These will be used for mounting the bat house to a post or building. The holes should be located in the center and 2" from the edge.

Step 10

The bat house can be mounted on a 4×4 post or the side of a building using 3" long, ⁵⁄₁₆" screws or lag bolts. A large washer (fender washer) is recommended to protect the wood. Mounting on trees is not recommended because they have proven to be the least successful location for bat houses.

bat house owner, the best you can do is select a good design and place your bat house in the most ideal location available. Here are some suggestions:

1. If you have bats in your area, observe their normal flight patterns and position the bat house where the bats will most likely see it or detect the crevices with echolocation. Most bats prefer to drop a few feet as they exit from a roost, so make sure there is ample space below the bat house. Likewise, the area leading away from the bat house should be open and not cluttered or blocked by tree branches and buildings.

2. Colonial bats prefer warm roost sites, so a bat house should be located where it will receive at least four to six hours of sunlight. In Florida, this is not as critical as in northern states, but areas that are shaded during the day should be avoided.

3. There are essentially three alternatives for mounting a bat house: on a post, on the side of a building, or on a tree. Bat houses located on posts have proven to be the most successful. They also offer more flexibility in where they can be located. Bat houses mounted on the sides of buildings also have a good chance of acquiring bats, but here the concern is that droppings may start showing up on the wall of the building. Also, Brazilian free-tailed bats have a scent gland that produces a strong musky odor. A colony of these bats close to a window, door, or patio might be objectionable. For these reasons, garages, barns, and sheds work best for mounting bat houses. Bat houses mounted on trees have proven to be the least successful. This is likely one of the reasons that early bat houses were not very successful. Most people would mount them on trees, where they would be shaded much of the day. Many colonial bats roost in dead trees, but dead trees have no foliage, and the sun warms the roost during the day. If you choose to mount a bat house on a tree, it should be oriented in a way that keeps branches from obstructing the entrance and allows as much sunlight as possible on the bat house during the day. It is recommended that predator guards be added to prevent snakes, raccoons, cats, etc. from gaining access to the colony.

4. The higher a bat house is mounted, the greater the chance it will be occupied. The bat house should be located at least ten feet above the ground, which is about the height of the eaves on a single-story home. Bats have been found in lower roosts, but occurrences are rare.

5. If possible, locate the bat house near open fresh water. Bat houses on the edges of lakes, streams, and canals have proven to be very successful. Because of the high insect activity, bats often use these as foraging areas. They also fly low over the surface and drink by lapping up water as they pass. If there is open water in your area it is an advantage, but the lack of it does not mean you won't get bats in your bat house.

6. Be patient. Although we have reports of bats moving into a bat house

within a few weeks, it may be two or three years before bats move into a bat house. If bats have not moved in after several years, you may want to choose another location or add a bat house elsewhere.

How Do I Know If I Have Bats?

So, your bat house has been sitting out there for a couple of months and you are wondering if it has bats. One approach is to look up inside, between the crevices. If used sparingly, a flashlight during the day does not seem to bother the bats. If your bat house is mounted high off the ground, you may need to use binoculars. If you have bats, you will likely see little bat faces looking down at you. Sometimes it is difficult to see up into the bat house against a bright sky, so try it on a cloudy or overcast day. Another approach is to look for guano underneath the bat house. If bats have been there a while, this should be easy to spot. If nothing is visible, or if you are not sure, you can lay a piece of plastic under the bat house in the late afternoon and check it the next morning. The best approach, however, is to watch the bat house at emergence time.

Community Bat Houses

A community bat house is a large structure designed to provide roosting habitat for several thousand or more bats. We refer to them as "community bat houses" because they provide insect control for the surrounding neighborhood. They are also often constructed as a community project involving volunteers, local businesses, and financial contributors. An indirect benefit of a community bat house is that it demonstrates that the residents are concerned about the well-being of their local wildlife. Educational kiosks and programs at these sites can be used to inform the public about bats and their role in the environment.

Sugarloaf Key Bat House

The first community bat houses were constructed in Florida during the 1920s. Unfortunately, they were not very successful. Most were copied from a design that had proven successful out west, primarily in Texas. One of these remains today on Sugarloaf Key, in the Lower Florida Keys (figure 8.2). It was constructed by Richter Clyde Perky in 1929. The big mystery surrounding the Sugarloaf Key bat house had always been, where did Mr. Perky get his bats? Some say he brought them in from Texas; others say he imported them from Cuba; and yet another story relates that he brought bats in from New Jersey, along with a caretaker. Fortunately, Fred Johnson, the man who actually constructed

Figure 8.2. The Sugarloaf Key bat house, built by Clyde Perky in 1929 as a means of mosquito control for his planned development, was never occupied (photo by Cynthia Marks).

the bat house for Mr. Perky, shared his story in recorded interviews before he passed away.

During the 1920s, Florida attracted many an entrepreneur looking for a way to make a fortune, and Richter Clyde Perky was no exception. Perky purchased land on Sugarloaf Key and planned to build a major tourist resort. He arranged for a stop on the new Flagler Railroad, established a post office, and of course, named the area after himself (Perky, Florida). But there was one big problem on Sugarloaf Key: MOSQUITOES. Perky was convinced he needed to get rid of the mosquitoes if his resort were to entice tourists.

Perky had read a book titled *Bats, Mosquitoes and Dollars*, written by Dr. Charles Campbell of San Antonio, Texas, and after sending someone to Texas to meet with Dr. Campbell, he decided to construct a bat house on Sugarloaf Key. Dr. Campbell, at the time, offered a package deal consisting of a set of bat house plans and a crate of bat bait for $500. The theory was that once the bat house was constructed, the bat bait could be installed and would attract bats from miles around. It was known at the time that bats were in the area, since they were getting into the telephone junction boxes and interrupting service. So, it seemed like the scheme might work. Mr. Perky commissioned Fred Johnson, his superintendent for the area, to construct the bat house and install the bat bait.

Construction began on the bat house in early 1929. According to Johnson, the best materials were used and the total cost of the bat house added up to $10,000, which was a lot of money in 1929. Once the bat house was completed, the bait was ordered from Texas and shipped in on the Flagler Railroad. Following Dr. Campbell's directions, holes were drilled in the box containing the bait, and distilled water was added to activate it. Johnson added, "When the water hit the bait, the smell was unbearable."

The bat house was dedicated on March 15, 1929, with a strong odor and no bats. It was here at the dedication that the stories began regarding the source of the bats, and the first one was generated by none other than Perky himself. The dedication was quite an event for the area, complete with the Key West High School Band. Mr. Perky announced in his flamboyant style that he had brought bats from Cuba and put them in the bat house, but the mosquitoes ate the bats, and that's why there were no bats in the bat house!

A few months later, a major storm hit the Keys and washed all of the bait out of the box. When attempting to contact Dr. Campbell to order another shipment, they were informed by his son that he had passed away. The son told them he had no idea what the formula was for bat bait. So the bat house remained with no bait and, of course, no bats. (We guess the bait was probably bat guano from Texas.) In the interview, Fred Johnson indicated that he had heard the various stories of how Perky had acquired his bats, but said, "It just didn't happen that way." His closing comment on the topic was, "And that was the end of it. We never had any bats."

If you are ever traveling to the Florida Keys, you may want to drop by and take a look. The bat house is located on the southern end of Sugarloaf Key. If you are traveling south on US 1, turn right just past the Sugar Loaf Lodge, and drive back on Airport Road to the mangrove area at the end of the road. The bat house is accessible, but located on private land.

University of Florida Bat House

The most successful community bat house in Florida was constructed in 1991 on the campus of the University of Florida in Gainesville (figure 8.3). It consists

Figure 8.3. The University of Florida bat house, built in 1991, is now home to more than 100,000 bats (photo by George Marks).

of a large boxlike structure, supported 20 feet above ground on five wood poles, and topped with a gabled metal roof. The house measures 18 feet on each side and is constructed of exterior-grade plywood. Inside the house, there are 180 crevices created by plywood partitions spaced at varying distances of ¾ to 1¼ inches apart. Between the tops of the plywood partitions and the gabled roof, there is an open area called the attic. It was felt the attic would hold heat and help keep the bat house warm.

The story of the University of Florida bat house begins in 1987 when a fire destroyed Johnson Hall, which was then located on Buckman Drive. Johnson Hall had been home to nearly 5,000 Brazilian free-tailed bats. Having lost their home at Johnson Hall, many of these bats discovered that the design of the newly-constructed Percy Beard Track and Field Stadium was just the ticket. Others moved into the stands of the Ben Hill Griffin Stadium at Florida Field. The bats seemed to be enjoying their new homes, but many of the fans didn't care for the musky odor of free-tailed bats, let alone the gentle rain of guano as the bats emerged from their roosts during the evening games. It all came to a head in 1989 when Governor Bob Martinez complained about an odor while he was attending the Sunshine Games. University officials decided it was time to address the problem. The idea of a large bat house had been kicked around for some time, but could not get sufficient support to be funded. Now there was motivation to solve the problem, and it was decided to build a large bat house near Lake Alice. The University of Florida Athletic Association contributed $20,000 for the design and construction of the bat house, and another $10,000 for relocating the bats to their new home and bat-proofing the old roost sites. Everyone realized, of course, that this would be no small task.

In September 1991, the tennis complex at the track and field stadium and the stands at Florida Field were fitted with bat excluders. The excluders allowed the bats to leave the roost, but prevented them from returning. Approximately 3,000 bats were caught in cages as they passed through the excluders, and transported to the newly-constructed bat house. Unfortunately, the bats stayed only a night or two, and then left for parts unknown. The good news was that no one was complaining about a large colony of bats invading some other location, so they apparently found roosts that created no immediate problems. During the following years, as bats were excluded from other areas of the campus, they were transferred to the new bat house, but none chose to stay. A number of techniques were used by disappointed designers and builders in hopes the bats would remain; after all, it was a very nice bat house (at least the humans thought so).

Things started looking up in 1993 when, after another relocation attempt, a small group of seven bats remained in the bat house for a few weeks, but left in April. Then in January 1994, a bat was found roosting alone in the bat house. Others joined it over the following months, forming a colony of 200 by March, but they again left in April. The new tenants were mostly males who, for some unknown reason, decided to winter in the "big condo by the lake." In 1995, exciting things began to happen. The colony switched from a small group of males to a larger colony consisting of mostly females. In January there were 200; in February, 1,000; in March, 2,000; in April, 3,000. The first bat pup was found on May 26, 1995, confirming the presence of a maternity colony. In 1996, the colony contained an estimated 10,000 bats; in 1997, 60,000; and in 1998, 70,000. As of August 2001, the colony contained more than 100,000 bats.

A number of things have been learned from the University of Florida bat house. The bats seemed to prefer the smaller ¾-inch crevices, and occupied them first. Persuasion techniques used to attract bats, such as adding bat guano, playing recordings of colony roost chatter, and placing a black light on a pole near the bat house to attract insects did not seem to help. Repeated attempts to move bats into the bat house from other areas failed. The bats would remain at most for a few days and then abandon the roost. Over the first few years of occupancy, the colony size increased much more rapidly than would be expected from reproduction, and at the same time, bat nuisance problems declined on

Figure 8.4. The Tallahassee bat house was built by volunteers as a community project in 1999 (photo by George Marks).

campus. From this, it has been speculated that the bats were attracting others from surrounding areas to the bat house.

If you would like to see the bat house, it is located on Museum Road on the University of Florida campus, across from Lake Alice. As you are proceeding west on Museum Road, there is a parking area located a short distance past the bat house, on the same side of the road. If you wish to watch the emergence, you should arrive by sunset. Clear, warm evenings are best. Benches and an informational kiosk have been provided for visitors.

A Flourish of Community Bat Houses

Encouraged by the success of the University of Florida bat house, bat enthusiasts have constructed a number of community bat houses in Florida. The Tallahassee bat house (figure 8.4) is an example of how community bat houses can be made to look attractive and enhance an unused public area, in this case, a retention pond. The bat house was constructed in 1999, and although there is some evidence of occasional occupancy, a colony of bats has not yet taken up residence. If you would like to visit this bat house, it is located behind the Tallahassee Mall, which is on US 27 (Monroe Street), about a mile south of I-10.

If you are considering a community bat house for your area, here is a list of benefits that can be used to help convince others to support the project. Community bat houses can:

Provide supplemental insect control for the area
Provide a site for environmental education programs
Provide habitat for bats excluded from nearby buildings
Provide a place for families to watch bat emergences in the evening
Offer an opportunity for the community to work together
Demonstrate that the community cares about conserving wildlife

Appendix B provides a listing of community bat houses in Florida accessible by the public. Some of these were constructed because exclusions of large bat colonies were taking place nearby, others were constructed as community projects led by volunteers who wanted to provide a roost for bats in their area. The bat houses listed as being on preserved lands have proven quite successful. Of the urban bat houses, none has yet experienced the success of the University of Florida bat house. Most of the bat houses listed are relatively new, and in time may yet acquire a colony. The status of several of these is tracked on the Florida Bat Conservancy website and you may wish to check for an up-to-date report.

~

The success of backyard bat houses over the past several years has provided a bright spot in bat conservation. They are serving as alternative roost habitat for urban bats and helping to increase public awareness. The success of the University of Florida bat house provides encouragement for the construction of larger community bat houses. We are, however, waiting to see if other community bat houses will begin to experience the same level of success.

9

Bats and Human Health

While the benefits of bats far outweigh any public health threat, there are two diseases of concern to humans: rabies and histoplasmosis. The threat of rabies has often been grossly exaggerated; nevertheless, it is fatal, and proper precautions to prevent it must be taken seriously. Histoplasmosis, while of little consequence to most people, can, in rare cases, cause serious illness. The purpose of this chapter is to provide an objective overview of the risks and consequences of these two diseases. Anyone desiring more detailed information or requiring medical information is advised to contact a medical practitioner or their local health department. By putting the risk of these two diseases in proper perspective while continuing to educate the public about rabies precautions, humans can enjoy watching bats in the evening skies, and bat colonies can continue to play an important role in Florida ecosystems.

Rabies: What Is the Risk?

Rabies is a viral disease that affects the central nervous system of humans and other mammals, ultimately causing death. At one time, the number of deaths in the United States due to rabies was quite high and due mainly to dog bites, but as a result of aggressive pet vaccination programs, the number of human deaths has dropped to one or two per year. Because pet vaccination programs have been successful, rabies cases are now mostly due to encounters with wildlife.

Scientific studies in which random samples of bats were tested showed that less than one-half of one percent of the bats in the study had the disease. This differs considerably from the percentages published by governmental agencies, which often indicate that approximately 10 percent of the bats tested are found to be positive for rabies. This is a case where accurate numbers can be misleading. The bats that are tested by governmental agencies are bats that have been found on the ground or in abnormal locations. These are more likely to be sick bats, a very biased sample. The results do, however, point out that people should not handle bats, because the ones they are most likely to encounter (i.e., on the ground or in other unnatural locations) have a higher probability of being rabid.

Bats are not asymptomatic carriers of the rabies virus; that is, they do not contract the disease and carry it around unaffected, transmitting it to others. Like some mammals, however, they can harbor it for many months. Harboring the disease means the virus is dormant within their system. During this period of time, they cannot transmit the disease. It is only when they begin to develop clinical signs, and the virus is present in their saliva, that they can transmit it.

Rabid bats usually die within several days after exhibiting clinical signs of the virus. Therefore, the period of time that a bat can transfer the disease is limited. Unlike other rabid animals, bats rarely become aggressive, and usually will bite only in self-defense. As the disease progresses, bats become paralyzed, often losing the use of their hind legs and the ability to fly. As a result, they may end up on or near the ground, where they can be found by humans and pets.

Because the disease is so fearful, it is easy to become overly concerned. The fact that rabies has often been the subject of horror stories and movies has not helped. Over the past 20 years, there has been an average of one death per year due to bat rabies in the United States. For purposes of comparison, the average annual number of human deaths attributed to dog attacks is 16; lightning, 90; food poisoning, 5,000; and flu, 20,000. Bats, like other wild animals, should be treated with respect, but we do not need to be fearful if they live in our community.

Rabies: How Is It Transmitted?

The rabies virus is transmitted by the saliva of the infected animal. The saliva is almost always transferred to the victim through a bite, but it can also be transferred if the saliva comes into contact with an open wound, or the mucous membranes of the eyes, nose, or mouth. A person cannot get rabies just by being near a bat or by coming into contact with bat guano, urine, blood, or fur.

People are usually aware when they are bitten by a bat and can take appropriate action, but bat bites are small and, in some situations, may go unnoticed, as in the case of a sleeping or incapacitated person. Viruses change over time and form variants of the disease. As this happens within a particular type of animal (bats, for example), the virus can be identified as coming from that animal. Consequently, it is possible to identify a bat virus as the source of rabies in another animal, even though the bat was never seen or found. In recent years, there have been human deaths from what has been identified as bat rabies although no bite was reported. Unfortunately, by the time the disease is diagnosed in a person dying from rabies, the patient is too ill to relate accurate information about a possible bite or exposure.

At one time, people became alarmed about the possible transmission of rabies through the air (aerosol transmission). This was the result of two individuals in separate instances contracting rabies while studying bats in Frio Cave in Texas, in the 1950s. Frio Cave is home to millions of bats. The atmosphere of the cave is very warm and humid, and the researchers were inside for several days. They handled large numbers of bats, worked under the bat colony, and incurred numerous cuts and scrapes, but could not specifically remember being bitten by a bat. Laboratory mammals exposed to the atmosphere of the cave in later experiments also contracted the disease without any evidence of a bite. It was concluded that infected saliva could become suspended in the water vapor of this warm and unusually humid cave. It is generally felt that aerosol transmission is extremely rare, can occur only in unique environments such as warm, humid bat caves, and is not a risk to the general public.

Rabies: What to Do If Bitten

If someone is bitten by a bat, it is imperative that immediate action be taken. The area of the bite should be washed with soap and water. Every effort should be made to capture the bat so that it can be tested for rabies. The next step is to contact the local county health department, county animal control department, or personal physician. If the bat was captured and tested positive, it will be necessary to immediately begin the series of rabies postexposure vaccinations. Fortunately, the shots today are not the ordeal they were in the past, and are no more painful than other vaccinations. If the bat cannot be captured, it will be necessary to receive the vaccinations, just in case. It is also recommended that if a bat is found in a room with a sleeping person (adult or child) or an incapacitated person (sick, impaired, intoxicated, etc.), the bat should be captured and tested. If the bat cannot be captured it will be necessary to decide whether postexposure vaccinations are advisable. In both cases, the local county health department or a physician should be contacted for medical advice. Rabies is a preventable disease, and the vaccines used today are nearly 100 percent effective when administered before illness occurs. Therefore, it is vital that medical attention is sought promptly following a possible exposure.

Rabies: Reducing the Risk

The best form of prevention is avoiding exposure. People who work with wild mammals should have rabies preexposure immunizations and follow the recommended guidelines for booster vaccinations. Unvaccinated persons should never handle a bat or any other wild mammal with bare hands. If a bat is found and needs to be moved to a safe location, thick leather gloves or a thick towel can be used as protection from bites (chapter 8). Children should be taught never to pick up or handle a bat or any other wild animal. It is important that pet vaccinations for rabies be kept up-to-date. There are a number of cases where bat rabies has been transmitted to cats, and the cats in turn have placed their owners at risk. Cats by nature attempt to capture small animals as prey, and sick bats make easy prey. Dogs can be curious and will investigate a bat on the ground, possibly acquiring a bite on the nose or paw. If a dog or cat has found a bat on the ground contact a veterinarian for advice regarding any necessary action to be taken.

Histoplasmosis

Histoplasmosis is primarily a respiratory illness caused by inhaling spores of the fungus *Histoplasma capsulatum*. The fungus is most commonly found in soils enriched by bird and bat droppings. It is prevalent on chicken farms, near large bird roosts (e.g. blackbirds, pigeons, starlings, gulls), and in caves with large colonies of bats. The fungus appears to flourish in damp environments where guano (bird or bat droppings) has accumulated and mixed with the soil over a period of time.

Ninety percent of all histoplasmosis cases in the United States come from the Ohio and Mississippi River valley areas, and some portions of Virginia and Maryland. Histoplasmosis is a relatively common disease. A study conducted by the U.S. Army indicated that in some areas of the continental United States, more than 80 percent of the population has been infected by it. Symptoms occur in only about 10 percent of the people infected, and appear as a mild, flulike respiratory illness. In most cases, the symptoms are so mild that a physician is not contacted. In fact, the vast majority of individuals affected are asymptomatic; that is, they exhibit no symptoms. Even in the cases where symptoms occur, there is usually no continuing long-term ill effect. Histoplasmosis is not contagious and cannot be transmitted from one infected person or animal to another.

The degree of illness from histoplasmosis varies greatly and can depend on the amount of spores inhaled, a person's age, and the strength of their immune system. In a small percentage of people it can progress to a chronic form of lung disease, similar to tuberculosis. In the rare and worst cases, it can spread to other parts of the body in a form of the disease referred to as disseminated histoplasmosis. It is the occurrence of these uncommon and rare cases that are cause for concern. People with weakened immune systems are more likely to develop disseminated histoplasmosis than others.

Bat caves appear to provide an ideal environment for the fungus. Because of this, many cavers around the world have contracted the disease, and it has, at times, been referred to as "cave sickness." In Florida, the disease has been associated with bats in only a few cases, all of which involved visits to bat caves, either by cavers or, in one incident, by a group partying in a cave and throwing guano at the bats roosting above.

Bat guano breaks down quickly into a dry, powdery substance. It is not dangerous and is usually left undisturbed after a colony of bats has been excluded from a building. If removing bat guano, wear a dust mask, as with any powdery substance. As a precaution, the guano can be lightly sprayed with water to reduce the possibility of airborne dust. If the fungus causing histoplasmosis is suspected, respirators capable of filtering particles as small as two microns should be worn. This, along with protective clothing and the proper cleaning or disposal of the clothing, can greatly reduce the risk of inhaling or transferring the fungus spores. Because the fungus grows best when the guano is mixed with soil in damp environments, it is unlikely to be found in the dry attics of buildings. To date, there have been no recorded cases of histoplasmosis in Florida resulting from bat colonies living in buildings.

Other Concerns

There are a few other health-related concerns that people often have about bats that should at least be mentioned. One is ectoparasites. Bats, like other animals, can acquire ectoparasites such as mites, but nearly all are specific to bats and do not usually transfer to humans or their pets. Another is West Nile virus. Bats can contract West Nile virus, but do not transmit it to humans or other animals. Like other mammals, bats do not transmit the virus back to mosquitoes.

The Centers for Disease Control and Prevention (CDC) has an excellent Web site containing detailed information about bats, rabies, and histoplasmosis. Anyone with an interest or additional questions is encouraged to visit it at www.cdc.gov.

10

Bat Watching

It is doubtful that bat watching will become a national pastime, but there are growing numbers of people who have developed a fascination for this unusual animal. Watching for bats can add an interesting ingredient to an evening stroll or a walk in the woods. Finding a place nearby where bats forage provides an opportunity to show children the real-life version of the creatures seen in scary movies. Environmental groups and nature centers often organize night walks to watch for nocturnal animals, primarily owls, but some are expanding those walks to include bats. This chapter contains information and suggestions that will increase your chances of seeing bats, help you interpret what the bats are doing, explain how to eavesdrop on bat echolocation with a bat detector, and even help you to conduct group bat walks.

When to Watch

The best time to watch for bats is just after sunset. Most Florida bats emerge from their roost about 15–20 minutes after sunset, but occasionally bats have been seen leaving a roost only minutes after the sun has disappeared below the horizon. If there are bats flying around, they can be seen silhouetted against the lighted sky. Spotting a bat in the early evening while there is still light will be helpful in attempting to guess its identity. As the sky turns darker, it will be more difficult to make out details, but you should still be able to get an idea of its size, wing shape, and flight pattern. Once the sky turns dark, bats become impossible to see. This is when a bat detector comes in handy. With a bat detector, bat watching can continue throughout the night.

If you are an early riser, bat watching can resume once again in the morning. Bats will attempt to be back in their roost just before the sun comes up. The sky becomes sufficiently lighted to see bats about a half hour before sunrise. In fact, early morning bat viewing is a good way to find a bat roost, because once bats have finished foraging, they will head straight for their roost. By following the bats, or at least noting their direction, you may be able to locate the roost. If you begin to see a lot of bats flying around in an area at this time of morning, you are likely close to a roost. They will often circle the roost site and take turns entering. Once birds begin to fly overhead, all bats should be tucked away in their roost, safe from harm.

An important factor in bat watching is the weather. Most Florida bats go into torpor for much of the day while in their roost. On cold nights, they will simply remain in torpor and wait until the weather warms up. It's not so much that bats don't like chilly weather as that there is very little insect activity on cold nights. Based on our experience, if evening temperatures fall into the 50s (°F), bat foraging activity drops off significantly. So, it is best to go bat watching on warm nights.

Rain has a similar impact on bat watching. If it's raining heavily in the evening, bats will usually remain in their roost. They may come out later if the weather clears up, but then it will be too late for bat watching. There is not a lot of insect activity on rainy evenings and, for the bats, it's also a lot more work to fly with wet fur. During a light rain, you may observe a few scouts emerging from a roost to check things out, but they usually return quickly, and the balance of the colony will remain inside until the rain stops. How many bats one sees on damp, misty evenings with light rain likely depends on how desperate the bats are to forage. If it has been raining for several consecutive nights, or if mothers are nursing their young, bats may still emerge to feed even on a drizzly evening.

Where to Look

The best place to look for bats in Florida is where there is a lot of insect activity. Of course, that's just about anywhere in Florida, which is good news for bat watchers. Some places have more insect activity than others, and that's where you want to go to see bats. Here are some good foraging areas to check out:

Small ponds and wetland areas
Rivers, streams, and canals
Mangroves and saltwater marshes
Edges of lakes and swamps
Tree lines, such as a forest edge or tree-lined street
Street lights and lighted ball fields
Golf courses

If you know of a bat roost, or can locate one, you are in for some great bat watching. You will not only enjoy watching the bats but will also learn a lot. For example, you can count the number of bats exiting the roost, determine their emergence time with respect to sunset, and observe how the emergence varies with weather conditions. During the early summer, you can try to spot any juveniles emerging from the roost. They will be slightly smaller than the adults and notably clumsier in their flight. Here are some potential roost site locations worth observing:

Old dead trees with cavities or loose bark
Palm trees, especially those with thatches of dead fronds hanging around
    the trunk
Areas with large oaks and Spanish moss
Barrel tile roofs
Bridges over roads and waterways
Bat houses

If you are at a roost site, there is a chance you will be able to see the bats before they take flight. This is a good time to identify the species. By using binoculars, you can often get a sufficiently good look to make an identification. Remember, if you are observing a colony of bats, then your choices are among Florida's colonial species. For solitary bats, the habitat type and geographic location also provide clues. The tables in chapter 4 should prove helpful. Occasionally, one or more species share the same roost. So, if you identify one bat, that does not necessarily mean all the bats in the roost are of the same species.

Figure 10.1. Canals like this are used as foraging corridors and provide good bat watching (photo by George Marks).

What to Look For

Identifying bat species in flight is extremely difficult, even for people who have worked with bats for years. In fact, the very best one can do is provide an educated guess. The only way to positively identify a bat is to see it up close. Even this often requires measurements and a careful inspection—something that should be done only by someone qualified to handle bats and who has had rabies pre-exposure vaccinations. Nonetheless, it is fun to observe and speculate. Here are some suggestions. First, check the range maps to determine which bats might be in your area. Also, you should note which ones are common, since those are the ones you will most likely encounter. Observe how high the bat is foraging. Decide whether it would be classified as a large or small bat. See if you can determine whether the wings are narrow or broad. This takes a little practice, because the wings are moving rapidly and their flight is erratic.

Here is a key question. Are you sure it's a bat? Actually, for first-time bat watchers this might not be a foolish question. In Florida, there are several bird species that forage for insects about the same time bats begin emerging from their roosts. So, it is important to be able to tell which is which. The birds most often mistaken for bats are chimney swifts (*Chaetura pelagica*). Their erratic flight looks a lot like that of bats, as they, too, forage for insects in the evening skies. The wingspan and body length of chimney swifts are about the same as some of our larger Florida bats, so size alone is not a big help. One possible clue is that the tail feathers of birds extend much further behind the wing. A proportionally smaller amount of tail membrane extends behind the wings of bats. Unfortunately, this can be difficult to discern while the bird (or bat) is flitting around catching insects. The most foolproof way of eliminating chimney swifts from the possiblities is to use your ears. Chimney swifts make a continuous audible chattering as they forage. Bats, on the other hand, make no audible sounds, since their echolocation calls are above the human hearing range. The one local exception is the Florida bonneted bat, found in south Florida. The echolocation calls of this bat, although faint to the human ear, are extremely high pitched and would not likely be mistaken for bird chirps.

Other, but less confusing, candidates are the various species of nightjars and nighthawks. The two common nightjars in Florida are the chuck-will's-widow (*Caprimulgus carolinensis*) and the whip-poor-will (*Caprimulgus vociferus*). The most common nighthawk in Florida is, as you might guess, the common nighthawk (*Chordeiles minor*), although in the Florida Keys one might encounter an Antillean nighthawk (*C. m. gundlachii*). Nighthawks are much larger than Florida bats. They have wingspans of 20 or more inches and body lengths ranging from 8 to 10 inches. They also have a noticeable white band under their wings. Their flight is not erratic like that of bats, and they usually swoop down to capture their prey, often making a loud roaring or whoosh sound as they dive. Oddly, another common name for the Nighthawk is "bull bat," but it's a bird, not a bat.

Bat Watching with a Bat Detector

Handheld bat detectors add an entirely new dimension to bat watching. It is best to obtain one that includes both a volume control and a dial for tuning frequencies. A good handheld bat detector will enable you to pick up the call of a bat 75 or more feet away. Bat detectors are somewhat directional, with a broad cone of sensitivity emanating from the microphone. For this reason, it is best to move the detector around in order to pick up sounds from various directions. Tunable bat detectors allow you to select the frequency you wish to monitor. Using electronic circuitry similar to that of radio tuners, bat detectors produce audible sounds of any noise made at the frequency to which the detector is set. All other sounds outside the bandwidth of the tuner are screened out.

The first thing to do when you begin your search with a bat detector is to make sure it is working. This can be done by turning it on, setting the frequency

Figure 10.2. Bat detectors can be used to hear bat echolocation calls while observing foraging activities (photo by George Marks).

dial to somewhere between 20 and 40 kHz, and rubbing your fingers together a few inches from the microphone. You should hear a rasping sound coming from the speaker. Yes, you've just listened to your fingerprints! Set the volume control to a comfortable level and you are ready to begin. Now you can watch for bats with your ears as well as your eyes. Begin by sweeping in the direction you would expect to hear bats. In an open field, this would be 360 degrees. Start varying the setting of the frequency dial in the range from 20 to 60 kHz. That should enable you to pick up the calls of any of our native bats, with the exception of the Florida bonneted bat.

Eventually you will hear your first bat. There is nothing that exceeds the thrill of hearing the first bat on your own bat detector (well, maybe a few things). Each bat call will sound like a tick on the detector. But now we must ask another key question. How do you know it's a bat? Well, the good news is, there isn't much else going on in the ultrasonic range. So your bat detector will likely be silent most of the time. There are some insects that make sounds encroaching on the ultrasonic range, and we do have some of these in Florida. For the most part, their noises range up to about 18 kHz, and can be screened out by moving the frequency selector up until they can no longer be heard, or by moving the detector in another direction. Also, insect noises tend to be a continuous roar, while bat calls are a series of individual ticks. The only other sounds you are likely to encounter are human generated. Try walking on dead leaves or dry grass with the bat detector turned on. It will be difficult for someone to sneak up on you while you are using a bat detector! Also, if you want to listen for bats it is best to keep your hands out of your pockets, because the bat detector will pick up the harmonics generated by jingling keys or coins. Opening candy wrappers and similar tasks will often generate ultrasonic sounds. These things don't frighten the bats, but they are quite annoying to those using the bat detector. If the sound is a series of uniform ticks (usually 4–9 per second for our common bats), then you are picking up bat search calls.

Bat echolocation calls are described in chapter 3 and the details won't be repeated here, but we will discuss how to interpret what is heard on a bat detector. If you are listening to bat calls while it is still light, you can observe the bat's behavior along with the associated calls. When the search calls are first heard, the bat is usually flying steadily and likely listening for insect echoes. When the call rate picks up, and this lasts only for a second or so, the bat has shifted into its approach phase, and you will see it quickly change directions as it chases the insect, but you will probably not be able to see the insect. Then, as the bat makes its aerial attempt to capture the insect, you will hear the feeding buzz. The sound of the feeding buzz lasts only a fraction of a second, but it is unmistakable. If you have never heard it before, it is a quick zipping sound. At this same instant, you will see the bat make a dive, loop, or turn as it attempts to capture the insect in midair. The bat will grab the insect in its mouth, its wing, or its tail membrane, and bring it up to its mouth. The bat detector will be silent for a few seconds as the bat devours the insect, and then once again, search calls will be heard as it looks for another insect. One can gain some indication of the amount of foraging activity in an area by counting the number of feeding buzzes.

Handheld bat detectors are not as sophisticated as the equipment described in chapter 3, but they can be used to make some inferences about the species foraging in an area. The most reliable clue is the frequency of the call. Begin by checking figure 3.2 and noting the echolocation call frequencies of bats found in the area you are surveying. The strength of each call is usually greatest at the lower end of the frequency range. Additionally, higher frequencies are attenuated more rapidly in the atmosphere and would be detected only if the bat were very close. Table 10.1 provides suggested bat detector settings for resident bat species in Florida. There are a few species of bats in Florida that have call frequencies sufficiently unique to make an educated guess at their identification. If you are picking up a bat in the 20–30 kHz range, it is most likely a Brazilian free-tailed bat. You will see from the chart (figure 3.2) that the hoary bat also issues calls that dip into this range, but hoary bats are rare and usually found

Table 10.1. Suggested Bat Detector Settings for Florida Bats

Common Name	Scientific Name	Setting
Big brown bat	*Eptesicus fuscus*	40
Brazilian free-tailed bat	*Tadarida brasiliensis*	25
Eastern pipistrelle	*Pipistrellus subflavus*	45
Eastern red bat	*Lasiurus borealis*	40
Evening bat	*Nycticeius humeralis*	40
Florida bonneted bat	*Eumops floridanus*	10
Gray myotis	*Myotis grisescens*	50
Hoary bat	*Lasiurus cinereus*	20
Northern yellow bat	*Lasiurus intermedius*	30
Rafinesque's big-eared bat	*Corynorhinus rafinesquii*	60
Seminole bat	*Lasiurus seminolus*	40
Southeastern myotis	*Myotis austroriparius*	50
Velvety free-tailed bat	*Molossus molossus*	30

only in the forested areas of north Florida. If you are in the Florida Keys and pick up bat calls in the 30–50 kHz range, it is most likely the velvety free-tailed bat. Another bat that is easy to identify by call frequency is the Florida bonneted bat. Its search calls are in the 10–16 kHz range. If you are within the geographical range of this bat, you can try occasionally tuning the bat detector to its lowest frequency setting, but some detectors will not pick up calls this low. What you need is a good set of ears. This is where you can put the grandkids to work!

Another clue is the sound of the call. Unfortunately, the sound of bat calls on handheld bat detectors varies from manufacturer to manufacturer. Even with a specific bat detector, the sounds of the calls vary as the frequency setting is changed and different portions and harmonics of the call are heard. To help overcome this, one could consistently use the same setting when attempting to make an identification of a given species. To further complicate the issue, we as individuals interpret and remember the highlights of sounds differently. So, the only way to use this approach is to actually hear the search calls of a known bat species on your detector and mentally note how they sound. This can be done by spending time at a roost where you can be assured nearly all of the bats are of the same species. Another approach would be to use your handheld bat detector on a bat field trip where someone with a system that plots the calls can identity the bats as they fly by. At the very best you will be able to make an educated guess regarding one or two species in your area. Nonetheless, it is a great challenge and a lot of fun.

Guidelines for Leading a Bat Watch

A bat watch or bat walk is a great way to get people back to nature. It is best to limit the size of the group to no more than twenty. Everyone needs to be able to hear the leader and, of course, the bat detector. Be sure to provide participants with a list of things to bring. For a successful bat watch, you will need flashlights, insect repellent, a bat detector, and if you are near a roost, binoculars. Keep an eye on the weather. If it's going to turn cold or rain, it would be best to schedule another date. Plan to have everyone arrive about 15 minutes before sunset. That will allow time for greetings, late arrivals, and small talk. At sunset, the leader should begin by explaining a little about bats, what to look for, and what might be heard on the bat detector. It is also a good time to talk about safety, including where to meet if separated, since the return trip will be after dark.

If you are leading a bat walk, pick an area you have previously checked out and confirmed has bats. If possible, plan your walk to pass by several potential bat foraging areas, such as ponds, canals, and tree lines. While walking, you can talk about bat echolocation, what bats eat, the benefits of bats, and the species in your area. You may or may not see a bat, but hopefully you will at least hear some on the bat detector. A stationary bat watch works fine if you are at a location where bats have been seen repeatedly. A boardwalk over a freshwater pond or saltwater marsh often provides some good bat watching. A roost site, on the other hand, is a sure way of seeing bats, but a few precautions are in order. Have the participants stand back from the emergence area. For example, at a bridge roost, do not stand under the bridge. A lot of activity close to the roost will likely delay the emergence; although the bats may eventually come out, it will be darker and more difficult to see them. If you choose to use flashlights to see the bats in the roost crevices, do it early and briefly. Shining flashlights on the roost will also delay the emergence. Normal human conversation does not seem to deter bats, so complete silence is not necessary, but loud high-pitched noises should be avoided.

Once the sky turns dark, bat watching becomes difficult. If you continue your walk, looking for owls or other nightlife, be sure to keep the bat detector turned on. You might pick up a bat at any time. If you have a high candlepower lamp, you could try to capture a bat in a beam of light by quickly turning it in the direction of the echolocation call. This works best if the same person is holding both the bat detector and the lamp. The light does not seem to alter the bat's behavior, so unless conducted to excess, this form of bat watching does not appear to disturb bats.

～

Bat watching can provide much more than entertainment. There is still a lot to be learned about Florida bats. The more eyes and ears observing bats, the more that can be learned. Bat watching can be an opportunity to contribute to the knowledge regarding Florida bats. For example, you can monitor a foraging area and keep a log regarding bat activity. At what time of day do the bats begin to forage, and when do they stop? How does weather affect foraging activity? How does it vary seasonally? Another interesting project would be to monitor a bat colony. When did the colony first appear? Is the population increasing, decreasing, or remaining stable? Do the bats stay all year, or do they return seasonally? What is the species? How does the colony respond to disturbances in the area, such as insect spraying or building modifications? This is known as "citizen science," and if done carefully, objectively, and with well-documented records, can be valuable in providing data for establishing conservation strategies for wildlife.

Appendix A. Comparative Tabulation of Florida Bats

Scientific Name / Common Name	Occurrence in Florida	Status in Florida	Roosting Behavior	Regional Origin	Wingspan (mm)	Total Length (mm)	Body Length (mm)	Forearm (mm)	Weight (g)
Family: Vespertilionidae									
Corynorhinus rafinesquii Rafinesque's big-eared bat	Resident	Uncommon	Colonial	Temperate	260–300	80–110	38–56	39–46	7–13
Eptesicus fuscus Big brown bat	Resident	Uncommon	Colonial	Temperate	320–350	87–138	53–81	41–52	11–23
Lasionycteris noctivagans Silver-haired bat	Accidental	Rare	Colonial/ Solitary	Temperate	270–320	92–115	57–70	36–45	8–16
Lasiurus borealis Eastern red bat	Resident	Common	Solitary	Temperate	280–330	90–123	51–61	35–45	9–15
Lasiurus cinereus Hoary bat	Resident	Rare	Solitary	Temperate	340–415	102–152	72–78	46–58	20–35
Lasiurus intermedius Northern yellow bat	Resident	Common	Solitary	Temperate	350–410	121–132	70–72	45–56	14–31
Lasiurus seminolus Seminole bat	Resident	Common	Solitary	Temperate	280–330	89–115	46–68	35–45	9–14
Myotis austroriparius Southeastern myotis	Resident	Common	Colonial	Temperate	238–270	82–87	48–53	36–41	5–8
Myotis grisescens Gray myotis	Resident	Endangered	Colonial	Temperate	270–320	80–96	41–57	40–46	8–10
Myotis septentrionalis Northern long-eared myotis	Accidental	Rare	Colonial	Temperate	230–270	74–96	41–59	32–39	5–10

Myotis sodalis Indiana myotis	Accidental	Endangered	Colonial	Temperate	240–280	73–100	41–49	35–41	6–10
Nycticeius humeralis Evening bat	Resident	Common	Colonial	Temperate	260–280	81–105	49–67	33–39	6–12
Pipistrellus subflavus Eastern pipistrelle	Resident	Uncommon	Colonial/ Solitary	Temperate	210–260	71–98	36–52	31–36	6–8
Family: Molossidae									
Eumops floridanus Florida bonneted bat	Resident	Endangered	Colonial	Tropical	490–530	130–165	84–108	61–66	34–47
Molossus molossus Velvety free-tailed bat	Resident	Uncommon	Colonial	Tropical	255–290	93–100	59–65	32–38	7–15
Tadarida brasiliensis Brazilian free-tailed bat	Resident	Common	Colonial	Tropical	290–325	90–109	57–74	36–46	10–15
Family: Phyllostomidae									
Artibeus jamaicensis Jamaican fruit-eating bat	Accidental	Rare	Colonial	Tropical	340–445	75–85	75–85	50–63	27–45
Erophylla sezekorni Buffy flower bat	Accidental	Rare	Colonial	Tropical	300–340	77–92	65–75	42–55	13–21
Phyllonycteris poeyi Cuban flower bat	Accidental	Rare	Colonial	Tropical	294–350	71–95	64–83	43–51	15–29
Phyllops falcatus Cuban fig-eating bat	Accidental	Rare	Solitary	Tropical	315–365	52–65	52–65	39–48	16–23

Appendix B. Community Bat Houses in Florida

Name	Year built	Nearest city or town	Location
Austin Carey Forest	2002	Gainesville	University of Florida, Austin Carey Memorial Teaching Forest.
Florida A&M University	2001	Tallahassee	Florida A&M University, adjacent to the band field.
Hardee Pipe (Concrete)	2003	Chiefland	Lower Suwannee National Wildlife Refuge, near North Loop Road.
Hickory Mound	2002	Perry	Hickory Mound State Wildlife Management Area. From Perry, go 20 miles west on US 98. Turn left onto Cow Creek Road and proceed 7 miles south. Drive around the dike to the walking trail, which has signs to the bat house.
Perky Bat Tower	1929	Sugarloaf Key	Traveling south on US 1, turn right just past the Sugar Loaf Lodge, and drive back to the mangrove area at the end of the road.
Phipps	2000	Tallahassee	Elinor Klapp-Phipps Park. Proceed north on Meridian Road (SR 155) from Tallahassee. Turn west (left) onto Millers Landing Road. Park entrance is on left.
Refuge Bat House	2002	Chiefland	Lower Suwannee National Wildlife Refuge. From US 19, south of Chiefland, turn west onto CR 347. Road proceeds west and then south. Bat house is near refuge headquarters.
Suwannee River Music Park	2003	Live Oak	Suwannee River Music Park. From I-75, take exit 451. Proceed 4.5 miles south. Watch for sign.
Tallahassee	1999	Tallahassee	John Knox Road stormwater retention pond, behind the Tallahassee Mall on US 27 (Monroe Street) about a mile south of I-10.
University of Florida	1991	Gainesville	University of Florida, on Museum Road across from Lake Alice.

Appendix C. Accidental Specimens Recorded in Florida

	Location Found	Date Found	Recorded by	Specimen Location	Specimen Number
Northern Accidentals					
Lasionycteris noctivagans	Santa Rosa County, near Jay	9/6/1985	Larry Brown	USNM	568099
Lasionycteris noctivagans	Monroe County, Bahia Honda Key	1996	Phil Frank	AMNH	269826
Myotis septentrionalis	Jackson County, Old Indian Cave	10/31/1954	Dale Rice	FMNH	1043
Myotis sodalis	Jackson County, Old Indian Cave	10/14/1955	William Jennings	FMNH	UF 560
Myotis sodalis	Jackson County, Old Indian Cave	10/14/1955	William Jennings	FMNH	UF 5192
Southern Accidentals					
Artibeus jamaicensis	Monroe County, Key West	6/6/1995	Phil Frank	FMNH	UF 31153
Artibeus jamaicensis	Monroe County, Key West	3/23/1996	Phil Frank	FMNH	UF 31154
Erophylla sezekorni	Monroe County, Marquesas Keys	5/10/1996	Elaine Wilmers	AMNH	269557
Erophylla sezekorni	Dade County, Miami	9/21/2004	Cynthia Marks	FMNH	UF 31196
Phyllonycteris poeyi	Monroe County, Key West	2001	Cynthia Marks	GAES	NA
Phyllonycteris poeyi	Monroe County, Stock Island	11/16/2002	Cynthia Marks	FMNH	UF 30983
Phyllops falcatus	Monroe County, Stock Island	2/19/2005	Cynthia Marks	UM*	NA

Specimen locations:

AMNH American Museum of Natural History, New York, N.Y.

FMNH Florida Museum of Natural History, Gainesville, Fla.

GAES Glynn Archer Elementary School, Key West, Fla.

UM University of Miami, Miami, Fla.

USNM National Museum of Natural History, Washington, D.C.

NA Not available or not applicable

* Tissue sample only

Appendix D. Key to Florida's Resident Bat Species

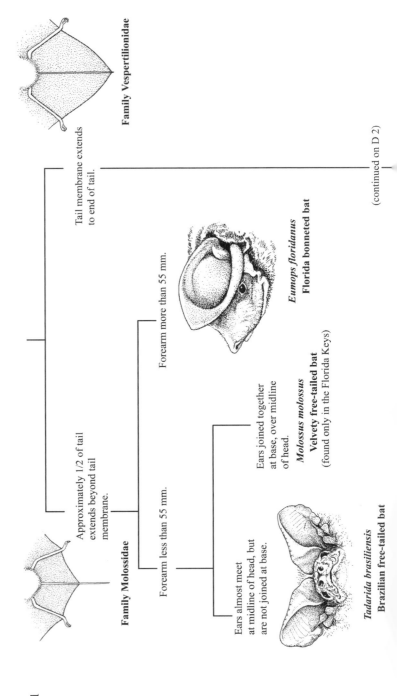

Tail membrane extends to end of tail.

Family Vespertilionidae

Approximately 1/2 of tail extends beyond tail membrane.

Family Molossidae

Forearm more than 55 mm.

Eumops floridanus
Florida bonneted bat

Forearm less than 55 mm.

Ears joined together at base, over midline of head.
Molossus molossus
Velvety free-tailed bat
(found only in the Florida Keys)

Ears almost meet at midline of head, but are not joined at base.
Tadarida brasiliensis
Brazilian free-tailed bat

(continued on D 2)

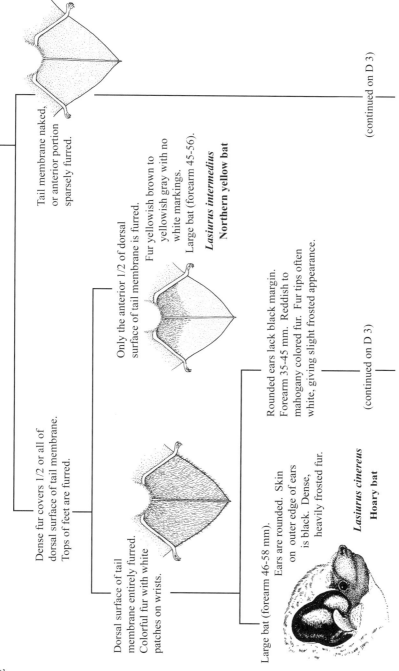

D 2

Tail membrane naked, or anterior portion sparsely furred.

(continued on D 3)

Only the anterior 1/2 of dorsal surface of tail membrane is furred.

Fur yellowish brown to yellowish gray with no white markings.
Large bat (forearm 45-56).

Lasiurus intermedius
Northern yellow bat

Rounded ears lack black margin.
Forearm 35-45 mm. Reddish to mahogany colored fur. Fur tips often white, giving slight frosted appearance.

(continued on D 3)

Dense fur covers 1/2 or all of dorsal surface of tail membrane.
Tops of feet are furred.

Dorsal surface of tail membrane entirely furred.
Colorful fur with white patches on wrists.

Large bat (forearm 46-58 mm).
Ears are rounded. Skin on outer edge of ears is black. Dense, heavily frosted fur.

Lasiurus cinereus
Hoary bat

D 3

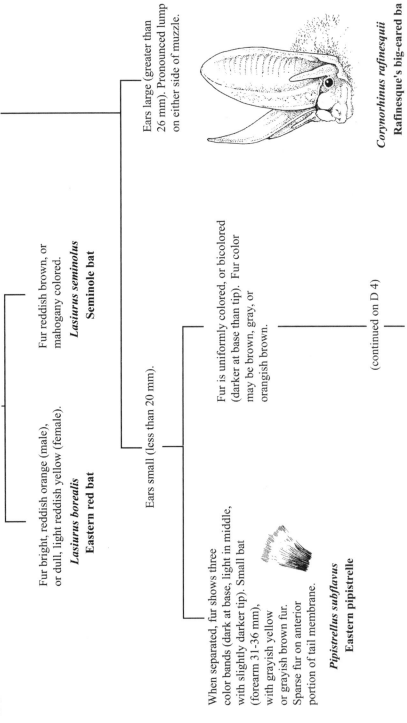

Fur bright, reddish orange (male), or dull, light reddish yellow (female).

Lasiurus borealis
Eastern red bat

Fur reddish brown, or mahogany colored.
Lasiurus seminolus
Seminole bat

When separated, fur shows three color bands (dark at base, light in middle, with slightly darker tip). Small bat (forearm 31-36 mm), with grayish yellow or grayish brown fur. Sparse fur on anterior portion of tail membrane.

Pipistrellus subflavus
Eastern pipistrelle

Ears small (less than 20 mm).

Fur is uniformly colored, or bicolored (darker at base than tip). Fur color may be brown, gray, or orangish brown.

(continued on D 4)

Ears large (greater than 26 mm). Pronounced lump on either side of muzzle.

Corynorhinus rafinesquii
Rafinesque's big-eared ba

D 4

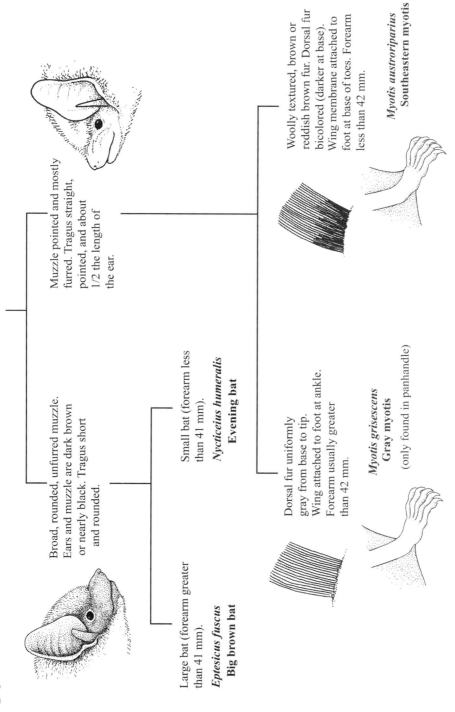

Broad, rounded, unfurred muzzle. Ears and muzzle are dark brown or nearly black. Tragus short and rounded.

Large bat (forearm greater than 41 mm).
Eptesicus fuscus
Big brown bat

Muzzle pointed and mostly furred. Tragus straight, pointed, and about 1/2 the length of the ear.

Small bat (forearm less than 41 mm).
Nycticeius humeralis
Evening bat

Woolly textured, brown or reddish brown fur. Dorsal fur bicolored (darker at base). Wing membrane attached to foot at base of toes. Forearm less than 42 mm.
Myotis austroriparius
Southeastern myotis

Dorsal fur uniformly gray from base to tip. Wing attached to foot at ankle. Forearm usually greater than 42 mm.
Myotis grisescens
Gray myotis
(only found in panhandle)

Glossary

accidental species: a general status category for a species occurring rarely and unpredictably in an area outside of its normal range.

adaptation: any feature or behavior that increases the ability of an organism to survive and reproduce in a particular environment.

anterior: located toward the front; the end closest to the head.

aspect ratio: the ratio of wing length to wing width.

bandwidth: the extent or width of a range of frequencies.

biosonar: the use of sonar by living organisms.

calcar: a structure made of cartilage that extends from the ankle toward the tail. It is unique to bats, and gives support to the trailing edge of the tail membrane.

camber: the curvature or convexity of a wing.

carnivorous: meat-eating.

chiropatagium: the part of the wing membrane that extends between the fingers.

Chiroptera: a taxonomic order of mammals comprising bats.

colonial: referring to bat species that typically roost in groups.

colony: a group living together in close association.

decibel: a unit used for measuring the intensity (volume) of sound.

dispersal: the movement of organisms away from their place of birth.

Doppler effect: the shift in the observed frequency of a waveform resulting from the motion of the source relative to the observer.

dorsal: toward the back, or upper surface; opposite of ventral.

echolocation: the process of producing sounds and using the information gained from returning echoes to navigate and/or pursue prey.

emergence: the evening exodus of bats from their roost.

endemic: pertaining to an organism that is found only within a particular area.

Eocene: an epoch lasting from about 55 to 37 million years ago; part of the Cenozoic Era.

exclusion/exclude: the process of evicting bats from a roost, typically a building, by using a one-way system that allows the bats to exit but not return.

family: a taxonomic group of one or more genera; the taxonomic level below order.

forage: to hunt for food.

forearm length: the measurement of the forearm from the outside of the elbow to the outside of the wrist.

frequency: the number of waveform cycles occurring per unit of time, usually per second.

frugivorous: fruit-eating.

genus (plural, genera): a taxonomic group made up of closely related species; the taxonomic level below family.

gestation: the period between fertilization and birth; pregnancy.

gleaning: a method of foraging in which insects are plucked from foliage, the ground, or other surfaces.

guano: the accumulation of fecal material from bats or birds.

habitat: a range of environmental conditions that can support a certain species; the place where the species is usually found.

hertz: a unit of frequency equal to one cycle per second.

hibernaculum: a roost used for hibernation.

hibernation: a state of reduced metabolic activity, in which heart rate, respiration, and body temperature are greatly reduced, enabling an animal to survive by conserving energy through winter months when food resources are low.

insectivorous: insect-eating.

juvenile: a young animal that has not reached adult size or reproductive maturity.

karst: an eroded limestone region with sinks, underground streams, and caverns.

keel: a flattened area extending from the trailing edge of the calcar of some bat species.

kilohertz (kHz): a unit of frequency measurement equal to 1,000 hertz (thus, 1,000 cycles per second).

lactation/lactate: milk production in female mammals.

maternity colony: a colony comprising primarily female bats and their young.

maternity roost: the site used by a maternity colony.

Megachiroptera: a suborder of the order Chiroptera composed of a single family of bats, the Pteropodidae, commonly referred to as the Old World fruit bats.

Microchiroptera: a suborder of the order Chiroptera; it includes seventeen families of bats.

migration: the regular seasonal movements of individuals or groups from one geographic region to another.

millisecond: one-thousandth of a second.

morphology: the study of the form and structure of an organism.

nectarivorous: nectar-feeding.

Neotropical: referring to the tropical regions of the New World.

night roost: a roost used during the night between foraging periods for rest, digestion of food, and social interactions.

nocturnal: active at night.

nose-leaf: a leaflike structure of skin and cartilage on the nose of some bat species.

Oligocene: an epoch lasting from about 37 to 24 million years ago; part of the Cenozoic Era.

order: a taxonomic group below the level of class and above the level of family.

plagiopatagium: the area of the wing membrane connecting the fifth finger, arm, body, and hind leg.

Pleistocene: the epoch that spanned from about 1.8 million to 10,000 years ago.

polyestrous: having more than one reproductive period during a year.

posterior: located toward the rear; the end farthest from the head.

propatagium: an expansion of skin forward of the forearm and humerus.

pup: a baby bat.

resident species: a general status category for a species that lives year-round in a particular habitat or location.

roost (*n.*): a site where one or more bats live during the day, or where they rest between foraging periods at night; (*v.*) to spend time at a roost site.

sanguinivorous: blood-feeding.

solitary: referring to bat species that typically roost singly.

sonar: the process of producing sounds and analyzing the returning echoes to obtain information regarding a target or the surrounding environment; SONAR: an acronym for sound navigational ranging.

sonogram: a graph used in analyzing sounds achieved by plotting frequency with respect to time.

species: the basic taxonomic category grouping organisms that can interbreed and produce fertile offspring.

subspecies: a subdivision of a species; populations of a species that, although able to interbreed, are considered distinct races, usually because of a geographical separation that over time has allowed slight physical or behavioral differences to develop.

tail length: the measurement from the base of the tail to the tip of the tail.

tail membrane (uropatagium): a posterior membrane connecting the hind legs and encompassing a portion or all of the tail.

taxonomy: the study of the names of organisms; the orderly classification of plants and animals according to their relationships.

temperate: referring to the midlatitude areas of the earth ranging between the tropical and polar regions.

torpor: a state similar to hibernation with reduced metabolic rate and lowered body temperature, often used daily by temperate bat species to conserve energy.

total length: the measurement from the tip of the nose to the tip of the tail.

tragus: a fleshy structure projecting upward from the base of the outer ear in front of the external ear opening.

ultrasonic: sound waves with frequencies too high to be heard by the human ear (above 20 kHz).

uropatagium: a posterior membrane connecting the hind legs and encompassing a portion or all of the tail; often referred to as the tail membrane.

volant: flying, or capable of flight.

wing loading: a measure of the amount of weight being borne per unit of wing surface area.

Bibliography

General Books on Bats

Altringham, John D. *Bats: Biology and Behavior*. New York: Oxford University Press, 1996.

Barbour, R. W., and W. H. Davis. *Bats of America*. Lexington: University Press of Kentucky, 1969.

Belwood, Jacqueline J. *In Ohio's Backyard: Bats*. Columbus: Ohio Biological Survey, 1998.

Fenton, M. Brock. *Bats*. New York: Facts on File, 1992.

Harvey, Michael J., J. Scott Altenbach, and Troy L. Best. *Bats of the United States*. Little Rock: Arkansas Game and Fish Commission, 1999.

Hill, J. E., and J. D. Smith. *Bats: A Natural History*. Austin: University of Texas Press, 1984.

Neuweiler, Gerhard. *Biology of Bats*. New York: Oxford University Press, 2000.

Nowak, Ronald M. *Walker's Bats of the World*. Baltimore: Johns Hopkins University Press, 1994.

Richardson, Phil. *Bats*. Washington, D.C.: Smithsonian Institution Press, 2002.

Schmidly, David J. *Bats of Texas*. College Station: Texas A&M University Press, 1991.

Wilson, Don E. *Bats in Question*. Washington, D.C.: Smithsonian Institution Press, 1997.

Other Selected References

Au, Whitlow W. L. *The Sonar of Dolphins*. New York: Springer Verlag, 1993.

Baker, Robert J., P. V. August, and A. A. Steuter. "*Erophylla sezekorni*." *Mammalian Species* (1978) 115: 1–5.

Baker, Robert J., and Hugh H. Genoways. "Zoogeography of Antillean bats." In *Zoogeography of the Caribbean*, 53–59. Special Publications, Academy of Natural Sciences of Philadelphia (1978) 13: 1–128.

Bain, James R. "Roosting ecology of three Florida bats: *Nycticeius humeralis*, *Myotis austroriparius*, and *Tadarida brasiliensis*." M.S. thesis, University of Florida (1981).

Belwood, Jacqueline J. "Wagner's mastiff bat: *Eumops glaucinus floridanus*, (Molossidae) in southwestern Florida." *Journal of Mammalogy* (1981) 62: 411–13.

———. "Florida mastiff bat: *Eumops glaucinus floridanus*." In *Rare and Endangered Biota of Florida*. Vol. 1, *Mammals*, edited by Stephen R. Humphrey, 216–23. Gainesville: University Press of Florida, 1992.

————. "Southeastern big-eared bat, *Plecotus rafinesquii macrotus*." In *Rare and Endangered Biota of Florida*. Vol. 1, *Mammals*, edited by Stephen R. Humphrey, 287–93. Gainesville: University Press of Florida, 1992.

Best, T. L., W. M. Kiser, and J. C. Rainey. "*Eumops glaucinus*." *Mammalian Species* (1997) 551: 1–6.

Brass, Danny A. *Rabies in Bats: Natural History and Public Health Implications*. Ridgefield, Conn.: Livia Press, 1994.

Brown, Larry N. "First occurrence of the little brown bat, *Myotis lucifugus*, in Florida." *Florida Scientist* (1985) 48: 200–201.

————. "First record of the silver-haired bat, *Lasionycteris noctivagans* (LeConte) in Florida." *Florida Scientist* (1986) 49: 167–68.

Brown, Larry N., and Curtis K. Brown. "First record of the eastern big-eared bat (*Plecotus rafinesquii*) in southern Florida." *Florida Scientist* (1993) 56: 63–64.

Campbell, Charles A. R. *Bats, Mosquitoes and Dollars*. Boston: The Stratford Company, 1925.

Centers for Disease Control and Prevention. "Rabies." <www.cdc.gov/ncidod/dvrd/rabies>, accessed 1 September 2004.

————. "Histoplasmosis: Protecting workers at risk." National Institute for Occupational Health and Safety publication (1997) 97–146. <www.cdc.gov/niosh/9714eng.html>, accessed 2 September 2004.

————. "Dog-bite-related fatalities 1995–1996." *Morbidity and Mortality Weekly Report* (1997) 46(21): 463–66.

Chadwick, Douglas H. "A mine of its own." *Smithsonian Magazine* (2004) May: 26–27.

Chen, Ellen, and J. F. Gerber. "Climate." In *Ecosystems of Florida*, edited by Ronald L. Myers and John J. Ewel, 11–34. Orlando: University of Central Florida Press, 1991.

Constantine, Denny G. "Health precautions for bat researchers." In *Ecological and Behavioral Methods for the Study of Bats*, edited by Thomas H. Kunz, 491–528. Washington, D.C.: Smithsonian Institution Press, 1988.

Cryan, Paul M. "Seasonal distribution of migratory tree bats (*Lasiurus* and *Lasionycteris*) in North America." *Journal of Mammalogy* (2003) 84: 579–93.

Davis, W. H., and C. L. Rippy. "Distribution of *Myotis lucifugus* and *Myotis austroriparius* in the southeastern United States." *Journal of Mammalogy* (1968) 49: 113–17.

Engstrom, Mark D., and Fiona A. Reid. "What's in a name?" *Bats* (2003) 21(1): 1–5.

Ewel, John J. "Introduction." In *Ecosystems of Florida*, edited by Ronald L. Myers and John J. Ewel, 3–10. Orlando: University of Central Florida Press, 1991.

Fenton, M. Brock. "Sound waves." *Bats* (2002) 20(1): 1–4.

————. "Seeing in the dark." *Bats* (1991) 9(2): 9–13.

Fenton, M. Brock, and Robert M. R. Barclay. "*Myotis lucifugus*." *Mammalian Species* (1980) 142: 1–8.

Fitch, John H., and Karl A. Shump, Jr. "*Myotis keenii*." *Mammalian Species* (1979) 121: 1–3.

Fleming, Theodore H., and Peggy Eby. "Ecology of bat migration." In *Bat Ecology*, edited by Thomas H. Kunz and M. Brock Fenton, 156–208. Chicago: University of Chicago Press, 2003.

Frank, Philip A. "First record of *Artibeus jamaicensis* Leach (1821) from the United States." *Florida Scientist* (1997) 60: 37–39.

———. "*Molossus molossus tropidorhynchus* Gray (1839) from the United States." *Journal of Mammalogy* (1997) 78: 103–5.

Fujita, Marty S., and Thomas H. Kunz. "*Pipistrellus subflavus*." *Mammalian Species* (1984) 228: 1–6.

Glover, Kenneth V. "Bats at the University of Florida." Unpublished report, Environmental Health and Safety Division, University of Florida, 1998.

Gore, Jeffrey A. "Gray bat: *Myotis grisescens*." In *Rare and Endangered Biota of Florida*. Vol. 1, *Mammals*, edited by Stephen R. Humphrey, 63–70. Gainesville: University Press of Florida, 1992.

Gore, Jeffrey A., and Julie A. Hovis. "Status and conservation of southeastern myotis maternity colonies in Florida caves." *Florida Scientist* (1998) 61: 160–70.

Gore, Jeffrey A., and Karl R. Studenroth Jr. "Status and management of bats roosting in bridges in Florida." Draft final report. Florida Department of Transportation, Research Project BD433 (2004).

Greenhall, Arthur M. "House bat management." U.S. Fish and Wildlife Service, *Resource Publication* (1982): 143.

Greenhall, Arthur M., and S. C. Frantz. "Bats: Prevention and control of wildlife damage." Publication D5-D24. Lincoln: University of Nebraska, 1994.

Griffin, Donald R. *Listening in the Dark*. New Haven, Conn.: Yale University Press, 1958.

Handley, Charles O., Don E. Wilson, and A. E. Gardner. *Demography and Natural History of the Common Fruit Bat,* Artibeus jamaicensis, *on Barro Colorado Island, Panama*. Washington, D.C.: Smithsonian Institution Press, 1991.

Hristov, Nickolay. "Dueling in the dark: What moths tell bats in the heat of battle." *Bats* (2004) 22(2): 10–13.

Humphrey, Stephen R., and L. N. Brown. "Report of a new bat (Chiroptera: *Artibeus jamaicensis*) in the United States is erroneous." *Florida Scientist* (1986) 49: 262–63.

Hutchinson, Jeffrey T. "Bats of the sub-tropical climate of Martin and St. Lucie Counties, southeast Florida." *Florida Scientist* (2004) 67: 205–14.

Hutchinson, Jeffrey T., and Richard E. Roberts. "Notes on the eastern pipistrelle in southeast Florida." *Florida Field Naturalist* (2001) 29: 54–55.

Jennings, W. L. "The ecological distribution of bats in Florida." Dissertation, University of Florida, 1958.

Jennings, W. L., and J. N. Layne. "*Myotis sodalis* in Florida." *Journal of Mammalogy* (1957) 38: 259.

Johnson, Fred L. Interview with Blair Reeves and Betty M. Bruce. Audiocassette. 18 July 1967. Monroe County Public Library, Key West, Florida.

Jones, Clyde. "*Plecotus rafinesquii*." *Mammalian Species* (1977) 69: 1–4.

Kern, W. H., Jr. "Bat exclusion methods." *Proceedings of Eastern Wildlife Damage Management Conference* (1997) 7: 139–48.

Kern, W. H., Jr., J. J. Belwood, and P. G. Koehler. "Bats in buildings." University of Florida Cooperative Extension Office. Fact Sheet ENY-272 (1993).

Klinkenberg, Jeff. *Real Florida*. Asheboro, N.C.: Down Home Press, 1993.

Kunz, Thomas H. "*Lasionycteris noctivagans*." *Mammalian Species* (1982) 172: 1–5.

Kurta, Allen, and Rollin H. Baker. "*Eptesicus fuscus*." *Mammalian Species* (1990) 356: 1–10.

Lawrence, B. D., and J. A. Simmons. "Echolocation in bats: the external ear and perception of the vertical positions of targets." *Science* (1982) 218: 481–83.

Lazell, James D. *Wildlife of the Florida Keys*. Washington, D.C.: Island Press, 1989.

Lazell, James D. and Karl. F. Koopman. "Notes on bats of Florida's Lower Keys." *Florida Scientist* (1985) 48: 37–41.

Mancina, Carlos A., and Lainet Garcia Rivera. "Notes on the natural history of *Phyllops falcatus* (Gray, 1839) (Phyllostomidae: Stenodermatinae) in Cuba." *Chiroptera Neotropical* (2000) 6: 123–25.

Menzel, Michael A., Diane M. Krishon, Timothy C. Carter, and Joshua Laerm. "Notes on three roost characteristics of the northern yellow bat (*Lasiurus intermedius*), the Seminole bat (*L. seminolus*), the evening bat (*Nycticeius humeralis*), and the eastern pipistrelle (*Pipistrellus subflavus*)." *Florida Scientist* (1999) 62: 185–93.

Morgan, Gary S. "Fossil bats (Mammalia: Chiroptera) from the late Pleistocene and Holocene Vero Fauna, Indian River County, Florida." *Brimleyana* 11: 97–117.

Nagorsen, David W., and R. Mark Brigham. *Bats of British Columbia*. Vancouver: UBC Press, 1993.

Parks, Pat. "Bat Tower." *Key West Citizen* 17 June 1971: 6–7.

Platt, William J., and Mark W. Schwartz. "Temperate hardwood forests." In *Ecosystems of Florida*, edited by Ronald L. Myers and John J. Ewel, 194–229. Orlando: University of Central Florida Press, 1991.

Rice, D. W. "*Myotis keenii* in Florida." *Journal of Mammalogy* (1955) 36: 567.

Silva Taboada, G. *Los Murcielagos de Cuba*. Havana: Editorial Academia, 1979.

Simmons, Nancy B. "Chiroptera." In *The Rise of Placental Mammals*, edited by Kenneth D. Rose and J. David Archibald, 159–74. Baltimore: Johns Hopkins University Press, 2005.

Shump, Karl A., Jr., and Ann U. Shump. "*Lasiurus borealis*." *Mammalian Species* (1982) 183: 1–6.

———. "*Lasiurus cinereus*." *Mammalian Species* (1982) 185: 1–5.

Thomas, Jeanette A., and Mersedeh S. Jalili. "Echolocation in insectivores and rodents." In *Echolocation in Bats and Dolphins*, edited by Jeanette Thomas et al., 547–64. Chicago: University of Chicago Press, 2004.

Thomson, Christine E. "*Myotis sodalis*." *Mammalian Species* (1982) 163: 1–5.

Timm, Robert M., and Hugh H. Genoways. "The Florida bonneted bat, *Eumops floridanus* (Chiroptera: Molossidae): distribution, morphometrics, systematics, and ecology." *Journal of Mammalogy* (2004) 85: 852–65.

Tuttle, Merlin D. "The lives of Mexican free-tailed bats." *Bats*. (1994) 12(3): 6–14.

Tuttle, Merlin D., Mark Kiser, and Selena Kiser. *The Bat House Builder's Handbook*. 2nd ed. Austin: University of Texas Press, 2005.

van Zyll de Jong, C. G. *Handbook of Canadian Mammals*. Vol. 2, *Bats*. Ottawa: National Museum of Natural Sciences, National Museums of Canada, 1985.

Viele, John. *The Florida Keys: A History of the Pioneers.* Sarasota, Fla.: Pineapple Press, 1996.

Wadlow, Kevin. "Bat Tower History Recalled by Builder." *Keynoter* [Key West] 28 Feb. 1982: 4+.

Walker, Bill. "What the heck is karst?" Florida Speleological Society. <www.caves.com/ fss/pages/misc/karst1.htm> accessed 24 August 2004.

———. "Basic central Florida geology." Florida Speleological Society. <www.caves.com/ fss/pages/misc/geoflorida.htm> accessed 24 August 2004.

Watkin, Larry C. "*Nycticeius humeralis.*" *Mammalian Species* (1972) 23: 1–4.

Webb, S. David. "Historical biogeography." In *Ecosystems of Florida*, edited by Ronald L. Myers and John J. Ewel, 70–100. Orlando: University of Central Florida Press, 1991.

Webster, W. David, J. Knox Jones, Jr., and Robert Baker. "*Lasiurus intermedius.*" *Mammalian Species* (1980) 132: 1–3.

Wilkin, Kenneth, T. "*Lasiurus seminolus.*" *Mammalian Species* (1987) 280: 1–5.

———. "*Tadarida brasiliensis.*" *Mammalian Species* (1989) 331: 1–10.

Wilson, Don E., and F. Russell Cole. *Common Names of Mammals of the World.* Washington, D.C.: Smithsonian Institution Press, 2000.

Zinn, Terry L. "Community ecology of Florida bats with emphasis on *Myotis sodalis.*" M.S. thesis, University of Florida, 1977.

Zinn, Terry L., and Stephen R. Humphrey. "Seasonal food resources and prey selection of the southeastern brown bat (*Myotis austroriparius*) in Florida." *Florida Scientist* (1981) 44: 81–90.

Index

Cynthia S. Marks and George E. Marks have been working with bats in Florida since 1989. In 1994, they founded the Florida Bat Center (now the Florida Bat Conservancy), a nonprofit organization dedicated to bat conservation in Florida. They, along with volunteers of the organization, have presented hundreds of educational programs on bats, worked with state and local agencies on bat conservation projects, rescued and cared for injured and orphaned bats, helped home and business owners with bats in their buildings, and studied bat distributions and behaviors throughout Florida.